The Grass Roots of Art

by the same author

*

COLLECTED POEMS
THE END OF A WAR
THE TRUE VOICE OF FEELING
COLLECTED ESSAYS IN LITERARY CRITICISM
PHASES OF ENGLISH POETRY
COLERIDGE AS CRITIC
WORDSWORTH
ANNALS OF INNOCENCE AND EXPERIENCE
ANARCHY AND ORDER
THE PHILOSOPHY OF MODERN ART
EDUCATION THROUGH ART
ART AND INDUSTRY
ART AND SOCIETY
ART NOW
THE MEANING OF ART
KLEE (INTRODUCTION AND NOTES BY)
GAUGUIN (INTRODUCTION AND NOTES BY)

*

with other publishers

THE GREEN CHILD
A COAT OF MANY COLOURS
ENGLISH PROSE STYLE
THE POLITICS OF THE UNPOLITICAL
EDUCATION FOR PEACE

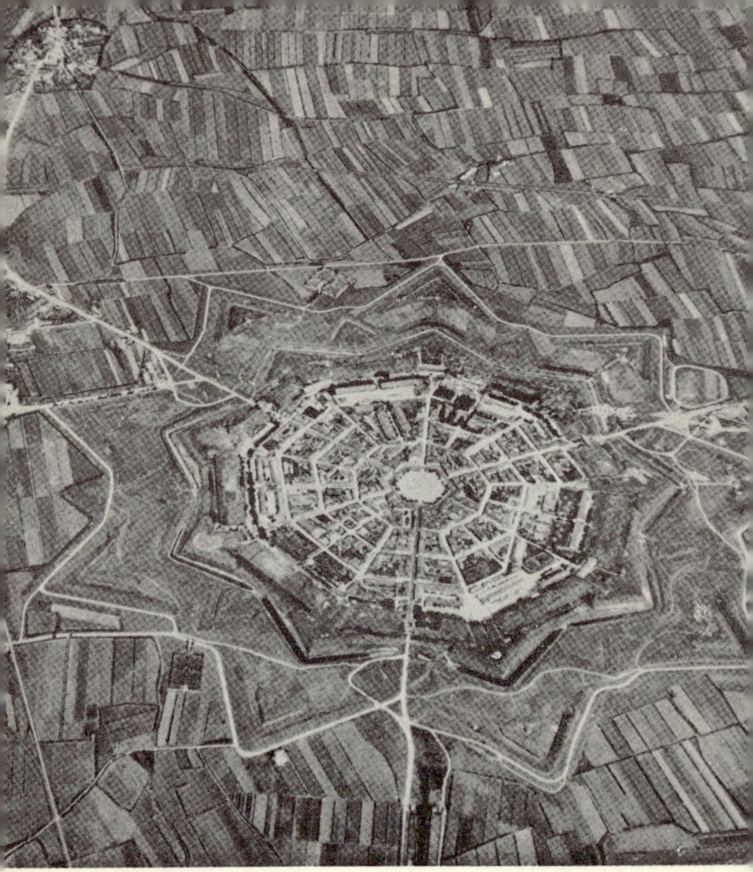

The Grass Roots of Art

HERBERT READ

Lectures on the Social Aspects

of Art in an Industrial Age

Meridian Books

THE WORLD PUBLISHING COMPANY

Cleveland and New York

A MERIDIAN BOOK
Published by The World Publishing Company
2231 West 110th Street, Cleveland 2, Ohio
First Meridian printing March 1961
Second printing January 1964

Reprinted by arrangement with Wittenborn and Company.
Printed in the United States of America 2MWP164

Contents

Author's Note

Earlier editions of this book (not identical with one another) were published in New York (Wittenborn, Schultz, Inc.) in 1946 and in London (Lindsay Drummond, Ltd.) in 1947. The present edition has been revised and expanded by the addition of two lectures. Four of the lectures were given as the Woodward and Trowbridge Memorial Lectures at Yale University in the Spring of 1946 (Nos. II, III, V and VII). The fourth lecture was an Annual Foundation Lecture delivered at Bretton Hall, Wakefield, at the invitation of the County Council of the West Riding of Yorkshire Education Committee in May, 1953. The sixth lecture was delivered to the Town and Country Planning Association, London, 1943.

Illustrations

will be found after page 96

Preface

Of this joy in living, there is greater proof in Italy than elsewhere. Buildings, pictures, and sculpture seem to be born, like the flowers by the roadside, to sing themselves into being. Approached in the spirit of their conception, they inspire us with the very music of life.

No really Italian building seems ill at ease in Italy. All are happily content with what ornament and colour they carry, as naturally as the rocks and trees and garden slopes which are one with them. Wherever the cypress rises, like the touch of a magician's wand, it resolves all into a composition harmonious and complete.

The secret of this ineffable charm would be sought in vain in the rarefied air of scholasticism or pedantic fine art. It lies close to the earth. Like a handful of the moist, sweet earth itself, it is so simple that, to modern minds, trained in intellectual gymnastics, it would seem unrelated to great purposes. It is so close that almost universally it is overlooked by the pedant.

With these words Frank Lloyd Wright expresses vividly the single idea underlying the various lectures that follow—the idea that art is in some sense intimately related, not only to the social structure, but even to the very soil and landscape of a country.

[1] Frank Lloyd Wright, *Ausgeführte Bauten und Entwürfe*, Berlin, 1910.

But that art is more than the craft and skill of peasants Mr Wright would be the first to admit. Art, even in its pre-historic or most primitive manifestations, is a discipline of the senses, a concentrated expression of social and individual consciousness, 'fine' in the sense that it is skilful, selective and intense. These values are now discredited as 'aesthetic' or 'formal', and there is an implication that they are to be despised because they merely give pleasure. But to deny the aesthetic basis of art is merely masochistic: is to deprive oneself of the pleasure properly belonging to a formative activity. Various writers—most recently Erich Fromm and Erich Neumann—have shown to what an extent the structure of modern society promotes masochistic and sadistic impulses, and so long as that structure remains intact, we must expect in art and literature movements that express the deep lack of community or brotherhood in our life. Art is a social bond only so long as it is aesthetic—only so long as it communicates pleasure by the means and rules to which our senses commonly respond.

Once this truth is accepted by contemporary artists, then the accumulated results of many years of technical experiment, pursued by many artists in many different directions, will be ready for synthesis. Technical research is perhaps not exhausted—the invention of new materials, the changing architectural environment, social factors of many kinds, will continue to call for experiment. But the technical discoveries of the past fifty years associated with names such as Cézanne, Matisse, Picasso, Braque, Chirico, Klee, Max Ernst, Naum Gabo and others, constitute a repertory of *means* the like of which has never before been available to the artist. In the art of music the historical critic can trace clearly the effects of purely technical innovations like polyphony or chromaticism; in painting, though the introduction of oil paints is a typical instance of the effects of an invention on technique, and the discovery of the so-called laws of perspective had a transforming influence on the whole art, it is only comparatively recently that experiment became 'free'. So long as painting, largely as a result of the discovery of the laws of perspective, remained tied to an ideal of scientific representation, so long form remained restricted, confined in phenomenal shackles. That this aim was based on a superficial and philosophically contemptible understanding of the nature of reality is obvious, but painters are not necessarily metaphysicians.

The formal liberation that we now enjoy is all-important, and many artists are satisfied with it. But the main release in modern art affects not its form, but its content. It is the imagination itself that has found freedom. If one likes to ascribe general movements to particular causes, then one may see Freud as the man with the master-key. It would be more exact, however, to see Freud as one of the liberated, as a leader in a movement that had been gathering force ever since the eighteenth century. In so far as that movement is personalist and subjectivist, it hardly makes for social unity. But society became disunited because it could not adapt itself to the individual's sense of his own integrity. A new social order will be possible only in so far as it provides for personal freedom. To provide for personal freedom is largely a question of providing the opportunity for creative activities.

I do not profess to know how real is the promise of such a social redintegration anywhere in the world today. If we try to get our own small field into focus, we then discover an opaque film over the central areas. A pattern may begin to emerge in some isolated spot—perhaps at some point on the periphery like Finland or Brazil (Figs. 11, 12). The older economies are amorphous—not merely because they are enveloped in war or threats of war: rather because they no longer provide those cells of good living which make for peace no less than for art. The definition of such an organic structure of society is a task for sociology, but among its characteristics we might distinguish physical limitations (no imperialism), a certain degree of economic self-sufficiency, political detachment, and social cohesion—characteristics found in the ancient city state, in the Greek colony, in the medieval borough. Each limited area of cultivation takes on a crystalline structure; or, since the process is essentially dynamic, let us say rather that it steadily revolves like a wheel round its relatively small urban hub (*Frontispiece*, Figs. 7–9).

Art is engendered by intensities and limitations, but none the less it is meant for universal consumption. The citizens of Beauvais built their cathedral out of a narrow regional zeal, but they invited the wonder and admiration of the whole Christian world. A local habitation does not imply a provincial mind. The best minds, that spent their days in the little worlds of Florence or Weimar, Königsberg or Cloyne, were universal. But it is difficult for a mind not to be shallow in the impersonal wildernesses of London or New York.

H.R.

March, 1955

I

The Roots of the Artist

When I began to consider the topic of this lecture, my first intention was to retell a story I have often told before—to tell it in different words and perhaps with a shift of emphasis, but still the old story of the modern movement in art, from its first origins in the romantic movement at the beginning of the last century, through impressionism, post-impressionism, cubism, expressionism and the rest, down to the latest phases of superrealism and constructivism. I would have presented my audience with a dozen labels or more, and an equal number of neat definitions. I might have gone on to show how, in spite of their modernity, such labels and prescriptions can be attached to various types of art in the past, and that there is in fact very little new under our contemporary sun. That might have reassured the conservative elements in my audience and at the same time flattered those artists who might thus find their wildest experiments justified by historical precedents. I would have pointed out that, though the history of arts is rich in forms, or diverse in modes of expression, a claim to anything in the nature of originality is to be suspected merely on grounds of genetic improbability. Millennia divide the earliest cave drawings from the painting shown in an exhibition to-day, but they represent but a brief span in the history of the human race; and they represent no change at all in the aesthetic quality of man's plastic vision. Mankind has evolved nothing subtler than the co-ordination of hand and eye which we find in the well-known cave paintings of Altamira, but this faculty is strictly comparable with the co-ordination we find to-day in a drawing by Picasso. Aesthetic sensibility has remained constant: what have changed, of course, are the habits and beliefs of the societies into which artists are born.

These habits and beliefs are a necessary part of human existence, and a recognition of the fact that they obscure, like so many shifting clouds, the clarity of man's plastic vision, does not justify what we might call 'aesthetic independence,' or 'art for art's sake'. Personally I would like to be a purist in art, just as I would like to be an individualist in ethics or an idealist in philosophy; but common sense compels me to a relativist or pragmatist attitude in all these matters. In art I am frankly a pluralist. Somewhere in the complex strand of human development there is a pure strain of aesthetic sensibility; perhaps, under laboratory conditions, it can be isolated. But usually it is intertwined with other threads, of magic, religion, science or politics; and according to the number and twist of these threads, the aesthetic sense is distorted and transfigured. But that is only half the relativist position. So far I have had in mind the objective aspects of art. But actually, as we know, the plastic vision passes through lenses of very different shapes. Every work of art is the expression of a personality or particular temperament, and though we can classify human beings with some degree of precision, and classify the modes of expression which correspond to the various types, we do not abolish the general picture of plurality and relativity. There are romantic artists in every classical epoch and classical artists in every romantic epoch. There were supperrealists in ancient Greece and constructivists in ancient Rome. There were impressionists in Egypt and expressionists in the medieval monasteries. No doubt an artist qualified in every respect to become a Royal Academician could be found among the pygmies of Central Africa.[1]

Relativism does not necessarily imply an absence of judgment. It can, of course, be maintained that all values, whether moral or aesthetic, are as relative as the experiences we call art, and in a sense this is true. The aesthetic canons of Puritanism or Iconoclasm have little relevance to the facts of art, in so far as these facts are an expression of the diversity of human creatures. Like fascism to-day, those religious movements were attempts to dragoon art—to control it from a centre and to impose uniformity on it. I personally take the view, which is heterodox to most people, that the more consciously moral or political values are imposed on art, the more art suffers. Art is spontaneous, the unpremeditated act of an individual, but always innocent. Where, then, does it find its scale of values? On what basis can we judge all the heterogeneous manifestations of art, if not by social or ethical standards? Where, if not in a moral code, shall we find a criterion of art?

The answer is, of course, *in nature*. There, absolute and universal, is a touchstone for all human artifacts. And we must understand by nature not any vague pantheistic spirit, but the measurements and physical behaviour of matter in any process of growth or transformation. The seed that becomes a flowering plant, the metal that crystallizes as it cools and contracts, all such processes exhibit laws, which are modes of material behaviour. There is no growth which is not accompanied by its characteristic form, and I think we are so constituted—are so much in sympathy with natural processes—that

[1] One has recently appeared out of the Australian bush—cf. C. P. Mountford, *The Art of Albert Namatjía* (Melbourne, 1944).

we always find such forms beautiful. The artist in particular, I would say, is a man who is gifted with the most direct perception of natural form. It is not necessarily a conscious perception: he may unconsciously reveal his perceptions in his works of art. Artists are to a considerable degree automata—that is to say, they unwittingly transmit in their works a sense of scale, proportion, symmetry, balance and other abstract qualities which they have acquired through their purely visual and therefore physical response to their natural environment.

But such a criterion is too normal and commonplace to be of much use in any comparative valuation of works of art. The more we insist that art should conform to the universal principles of the natural order, the more necessary it becomes to find other traits or characteristics to distinguish between one work of art and another. Let us admit that the work of art should conform to the so-called laws of nature: we have then only stated a *sine qua non*, a basis which, if that were all, would reduce all works of art to a monotonous uniformity. That is, of course, what really happens in those official academies where the teaching is based on the immutable canons of classical art. Hellenic art in its mature period did attain, as nearly as any school of art ever has done, an exact correspondence to the physical laws of the universe. But it was a *reductio ad ratiocinativum*, or whatever is the opposite to a *reductio ad absurdum*. The art lost its savour, its sensitiveness: it became a thumb-ruled copy of nature, and so-called classical art ever since has been a thumb-ruled copy of the antique.

The *vitality* of art lies elsewhere, and that elsewhere can only be, so far as I can see, in two possible places. It can lie in the cultural pattern of which the work of art is one detail—the whole, as it were, transmitting its vitality to the part; or it can be a quality of the individual artist, an expression of what we call his personality.

Here is, I think, a very important problem, with direct bearings on the cultural crisis of our time. Let me plunge straight into my argument and state the dilemma in its most acute terms.

We are all agreed, I assume, that our civilization is in a state of crisis. The system of laissez-faire capitalism, which has been the unconscious economic basis of our civilization since the end of the Middle Ages, has broken down, and various alternatives seem to present themselves. These take two general forms—either a continuance of capitalism with a planned control of its objectives, or the replacement of capitalist enterprise by some form of communal ownership of the means of production and distribution. It is not necessary, perhaps, to detail all the possibilities, but they are more various than some of our politicians assume, and the cultural patterns which would emerge from such diverse economic structures as, for example, the international cartelization of industry and the autarkic State control of industry would be totally different.

The question artists must therefore ask themselves is whether, recognizing the transitional nature of our period, they should wait for a cultural pattern to be determined by economic factors, and then more or less consciously conform to it, or whether they should adopt the only alternative policy and be content to make their art an expression of their separate and unique personalities.

Where, as in Russia, we already have a predetermined economic system and a cultural pattern corresponding to it, we find that the artist has very little choice in the matter. That particular cultural pattern excludes the individual solution and deliberately condemns all forms of expression which do not conform to the normal pattern. The individualist, in the U.S.S.R., is a pariah.

The first instinct of those who feel a little differently about the matter is to appeal to history. I am not sure that this is a logical course of action. We could undoubtedly find epochs of civilization in the past which had exercised a fairly strict control on the forms of cultural expression. The Arabic civilization is the most effective example. But the civilizations of the future will not necessarily correspond in their nature or mode of operation to the Arabic civilization, or to any model from the past. Indeed, I think it is more scientific to assume that they will be radically different. The present and future mechanisms of intercommunication and broadcasting in themselves sufficiently justify such an assumption, but the basic difference will be found in the mass productiveness of machine industry. For these reasons, if for no others, I think we must dismiss the appeal to history. History offers no solace to the individualist. It has been one long and unrelenting struggle for power, and power which, whether held by Church or State, by oligarchy or tyrant, has never tolerated the free expression of individuality. Liberty, unfortunately, is not a means to any form of political hegemony, and, as Lord Acton said in this connection, 'a generous spirit prefers that his country should be poor, and weak, and of no account, but free, rather than powerful, prosperous and enslaved. It is better to be the citizen of a humble commonwealth in the Alps than a subject of the superb autocracy that overshadows half of Asia and Europe.'

We need not, however, accept the pessimistic view that history has already exhausted all forms of social organization without achieving the liberty essential to the individual and above all to the artist. There are, for example, certain forms of federalism which have been projected but never tried. There is just a chance that some of these may be tried during the next phase of history. If, as General Smuts implied in one of his war speeches, we are to anticipate a world organized under three great power groups, then it occurs to me that there is a possibility that the holders of power within these three groups will be so preoccupied with economic and military affairs that they will make no attempt to control cultural affairs. Culture, no less than politics, has suffered from its liaison with the principle of national sovereignty. When nation competes against nation, national culture becomes a weapon of propaganda, a thing to hurl at your enemy or to bait a potential ally. The artist, along with the scientist and engineer, is conscripted. But if the world organization of power is to be given a wholly economic structure, then national cultures drop out of the picture, the artist is demobilized. It is a possibility which we can anticipate with some confidence. When General Smuts says that this trinity of power 'will be the stabilizing factor, the wall of power behind which the freedoms and democracies can be built up again,' we can, if we agree with him, argue that behind the same protecting wall the arts and literatures of the world will revive.

We therefore return to that point of view which finds the secret of the vitality of art in the psychology of the artist. If we could show that what we mean by a work of art is always and inevitably the product of the individual personality, and of that personality operating, naturally not in social vacuum, but in maximum conditions of personal freedom, then we should have established the irrelevance of all those cultural patterns which attract or menace us from the future.

The psychology of personality has been explored in great scientific detail by Professor Gordon Allport of Harvard University. In his Preface to his book on *Personality* he makes the following summary statement of the point of view I shall adopt, and subsequently brings forward ample evidence to support it. 'I do not deny,' he says, 'that personality is fashioned to a large extent through the impact of culture upon the individual. But the interest of psychology is not in the factors *shaping* personality, rather in personality *itself* as a developing structure. From this point of view culture is relevant only when it has become *interiorized* within the person as a set of personal ideals, attitudes, and traits. Likewise, culture conflict must become *inner* conflict before it can have any significance for personality. Why is it that in our times, when

Western culture is sadly disorganized, our own personalities are not correspondingly disorganized? The enthusiastic determinist might reply: They are. Our institutional anchors are lost and each of us is either drifting or breaking to pieces. But such a reply would be wholly unrealistic. Are personalities in fact any more disorganized now than formerly? Is there any sure evidence for an increase of insanity? It is doubtful. Certainly, it is impossible to hold that disorganization of personality to-day is *proportional* to the rapid shattering of cultural forms. Cultural determinism is one of the monosymptomatic approaches: it has a blind spot for the internal balancing factors and structural tenacity within personality.'[1]

If this is true, then not only is it nonsensical to assume, for example, that the modern art movement, as an expression of a decadent civilization, is already doomed, but equally that movement has nothing to fear from whatever pattern of culture is imposed on us in the immediate future. That, at any rate, is the thesis I want to maintain. Art, in the tangible form of living and creative artists, is not the by-product of a culture; rather, a culture is the end-product of the outstanding personalities of a number of artists. It is perfectly possible, as we know, to have a civilization without artists—ancient Sparta is an example, and modern Germany promised to be another. And even where a civilization, in the course of its development, coincides with the appearance of a number of artists, it has always been difficult to correlate the values of art with the values of the civilization. It is true that the greatest phase of English poetry coincides with the Elizabethan age, a period of national expansion, and another great phase of English poetry coincides with the Victorian age. But if there is some causal connection between these civilizations and their poetry, Victorian poetry ought to be infinitely greater than Elizabethan poetry, to maintain some correspondence with the infinitely greater extent and power of the

[1] *Personality* (New York, 1937), pp. 8, 9.

British Empire in the later period. And that is manifestly not the case. Naturally there must be minimum conditions of civilization for any kind of culture to exist, but those whom we recognize as great artists are never the direct embodiment of the general character or scope of a particular civilization. They are generated by some less portentous force, some more restricted ambiance.[1] The greatest dramatist of the nineteenth century appeared in the poor and remote kingdom of Norway; Spain, the most backward of European civilizations to-day, has produced our greatest painter. Even in a public art like architecture, I defy anyone to find an exact correspondence between the greatness of a building and the greatness of a civilization. The great medieval cathedrals may not be the expression of particular personalities in the same sense that a painting by Titian or El Greco is an expression of their particular personalities, but in the material sense the civilization which saw the building of these cathedrals was a mean one. That leads straight to the suggestion that the determining factor, in architecture and therefore in other arts, is a spiritual one. But a moment's reflection will show that this generalization, too, is wholly untenable. What specific spiritual force gave rise to the painting of Delacroix or Cézanne, or, for that matter, to the poetry of Shakespeare or Goethe? The evidence from music is even more striking. The great

[1] This complex problem has been clearly summarized by the Professor of Anthropology at Columbia University:

'We find that in all societies the personalities of the "average", "normal" individuals who keep the society operating in its accustomed ways can be accounted for in cultural terms. At the same time we find that all societies include atypical individuals whose personalities fall outside the normal range of variation for the society. The causes of such aberrant personalities are still imperfectly understood. They unquestionably derive in part from accidents of early environment and experience. In how far still other, genetically determined factors may be involved we are still unable to say.' Ralph Linton, *The Cultural Background of Personality* (New York, 1945), p. 152.

masters, Bach, Mozart, Beethoven, Berlioz, Sibelius, were not conscious exponents of the main cultural trends of their times. The most we can admit is that 'passion is the mother of great things' (Burckhardt), and that in periods of crisis, which by no means coincide with periods of greatness, unsuspected forces awaken in individuals. It is not that the individuals 'express' the crisis; rather, their highest faculties are called into being to overcome the crisis by the creation of new values, which are the expression of a personal vision.

If next we look at the positive evidence for the thesis that art is an expression of the uniqueness of a personality, it is overwhelmingly convincing. I am prepared to make, here as always, a distinction between public and private art, and to exclude, with considerable reserves, the whole art of architecture. The truth is that up to the Renaissance we know very little about the circumstances of building: the more evidence we dig out of the archives, the more insistently personalities emerge. Since the Renaissance the personality of the architect is stamped on every building of any artistic value, until we come to the functional architecture of our own time. (Even in this impersonal sphere, it is the great personalities of the movement, Le Corbusier and Frank Lloyd Wright, who are the dominant influences.) I do not wish to reduce all public art to private art. There are many great monuments, from the Pyramids in Egypt to Rockefeller Centre in New York, which have nothing private about them. What I would rather say is that the history of art simply does not make sense unless this distinction is borne in mind. The difference between the Sphinx and the famous head of Nefertiti is not merely a difference of degree, but also of kind. Certain works of art are, as it were, constructed by anonymous forces to express the might or majesty of a god or a king, or to fulfil the civic functions of a group of people. These monuments are classified as works of art, and I do not wish to dethrone them.

But constructed as they are in cold blood, with calculated measurements and estimated costs, what can they have in common with that still, small voice which issues from the innermost being of a poet or a painter in the intimacy of his own room, with the delicate accompaniments of silence and concentration out of which alone inspiration can be seized? The best gift a tyrant can offer a great artist is a prison, for there at least some of the essential conditions of artistic creation are possible. But though great works of art have been written in prison, because the mind of the prisoner remained free, liberty is nevertheless a privilege which promotes that energy of thought, fullness of interest and active curiosity which are necessary for the realization of an individual's integrity. We have only to consider for a moment the psychology of the artist in the process of his creative activity to make this quite clear.

It is difficult to select a representative case. If my thesis is correct, the personality of every great artist is unique, and we cannot therefore usefully analyse a *typical* artist. We may say with evident truth, that every artist must possess a vivid, sensuous organization, quick perceptiveness and ready muscular co-ordination; we can assume, as I have already pointed out, that from this physical disposition he acquires a special sense of form and harmony. None of these qualities has any relation to the form or content of the culture of his time. They are more likely to be due to differences in the germ cells with which the artist is born, or to be products of a specific endocrine constitution. They can be influenced by drugs such as benzedrine. But all this only amounts to saying that each man must have an aptitude for the task he undertakes. And in this sense there is no clear division between one type of man and another. The physical gradations of human beings are infinitely refined, and it is only at the extremes of the scale that one man may inevitably be destined to become an artist and another man as inevitably destined to become a dustman.

Many artists have left us revealing accounts of the creative process—poets like Keats and Coleridge, novelists like Flaubert and Henry James, painters like Van Gogh and Pissarro. Much analysis of works of art has been done by critics. In the end the specific quality which is isolated may, from a creative or dynamic aspect, be called *inspiration*: but objectively considered it is the precipitation of a certain *style*, and that style is peculiar to the individual artist. Style may include borrowed elements, but the value of a work is strictly proportionate to what we call the *purity* of its style, and by this purity we mean its irreducible element of personal grace or idiosyncrasy. 'The style of Titian' implies one thing, and '*in* the style of Titian' quite another. But the difference, to which historians of art devote the most exacting scientific analysis and the most intuitive perceptiveness, always resolves into something as personal to Titian as the timbre of his voice or the wrinkles on his brow. The style is the man himself, and although this aphorism of Buffon's has often been misapplied, it remains the basic fact about all forms of expressive communication.

I am pulled up by the word 'communication,' for there, according to some philosophers, the whole difficulty lies. Communication only takes place effectively within an agreed field of reference, in other words, within a cultural pattern to which the artist conforms. This may be the pattern set by an élite, or aristocracy, and then the patron makes the rules which the artist follows. Gainsborough, for example, paints portraits of his patrons instead of landscapes for his own pleasure, and paints them according to a conventional style. But the more recent theory, which Tolstoy put forward in *What Is Art?* and which has been given a more scientific or dialectical form by Marxist critics, insists that the artist should express himself in a style which is easily understood by the people. This may be a style of biblical simplicity, fit for peasants, which is what Tolstoy thought desirable, or may be a style of so-called socialist realism, which is current journalese spiced with political and scientific jargon. In any such case, the artist is being asked to depersonalize his style, to write in a basic language, paint in basic images, compose in basic melodies. That way can only lead to the impoverishment of art and really implies a sovereign contempt for the intelligence of the people. I would go to the opposite extreme, and maintain that every man's style, in the degree that it faithfully represents his personality, communicates its essential message. Just as normally we experience no difficulty in judging the value of a man's personality by his gait and expressive gestures, so we as easily accept and judge the value of an artist's style of expression. The trouble is that people no longer judge an artist by his style: they judge him by almost everything else—by his political or religious message, his social standing, his fame or the company he keeps. If he belongs to a movement, there will be a tendency to accept or reject his style as an integral part of that movement. Art movements in general, we may conclude, are legitimate in so far as they take the form of co-operative societies to aid in the free intercommunication of the personal styles of their members; illegitimate in so far as they impose on their members a common or doctrinaire conception of style.

Style, therefore, is effective in so far as it is free, and rather than attempt to evolve a common and easily digestible style, we should inquire into those forces which tend to inhibit the free expression of personality. We do not have to look far. In one direction we find an educational organization whose whole purpose is to teach the individual his manners, that is to say, his style; and in another direction we find the pervasive and anonymous pressure of the social or cultural pattern which has the same inhibitive effect on the individual personality. Whether that effect is conscious or unconscious, whether the drive to self-expression is sublimated or entirely repressed—these are psychological sequels we need not pursue at the present moment. I would like, however, to deal briefly with the educational aspect of the problem and to consider what measures we might take to develop within the existing social pattern a more positive and creative atmosphere.

I have devoted a whole book to this problem,[1] and the reader must excuse me if, in this brief reference to a big question, I make assumptions for which I have elsewhere offered the proofs. My general contention is that a system of education which aims at the creation of uniform standards of intelligence and, more indirectly, at the creation of a uniform pattern of culture, only ends by producing a widespread neurosis within the structure of society. The system of education, as it has developed in Europe during the course of the last hundred years and more, has concentrated exclusively on the cultivation of logical habits of thought and the orderly acquisition of facts. Memory rather than imagination has been its ideal, and its tendency has been to insist on an ethical concept of character rather than a balance or integration of the individual personality. Children have been treated as so much plastic material which could be moulded into static forms, instead of as extremely active centres of dynamic forces whose gears easily get jammed.

I must not devote any space to the negative side of the picture, but there is no doubt that a devastating indictment of conventional methods of education can be drawn up. The danger which then ensues is that the bad old method is discarded and no new metho d is put in its place. Freedom from the past tyranny may be achieved, but no alternative concept of discipline is established. If the children of the past have become neurotic adults because of the systematic repression and frustration practised on them by their parents and teachers, the children of the future are threatened by an equally bad

[1] *Education Through Art*, London (Faber and Faber), 1943.

neurosis because they have not been initiated into any principle of growth or integration.

The point of view which I put forward, as against the whole grammatical and logical tradition of education, is the Platonic doctrine which finds in the practice of art those regulative principles in virtue of which the integration of the personality can be achieved. Art is a *natural* discipline. Its rules are the proportions and rhythms inherent in our universe; and the instinctive observation of these rules, which come about in the creative industry of the arts, brings the individual without effort into sympathetic harmony with his environment. That is what we mean by the integration of the personality—the acquiring of those elements of grace and skill which make the individual apt in self-expression, honest in communication and sympathetic in the reciprocal relationships upon which society is based. Art, we might say, can make us completely human.

I must not let it be assumed, however, that art is a subject to be confined to the schools. We are gradually, I hope, getting rid of the fallacy that the process of education can be confined within any special institutions. Education is the continuous process of the adjustment of the individual to his environment; and if an individual ever claims to be completely educated, it merely indicates that he is in need of a change of scene. But a man who had retained the innocent eye of childhood would never make such a claim. To his ever fresh sensibility the world is reborn every day. 'Your enjoyment of the world is never right,' as Traherne wrote, 'till every morning you awake in Heaven; see yourself in your Father's Palace; and look upon the skies, the earth, and the air as Celestial Joys: having such a reverend esteem of all, as if you were among the Angels. . . . You never enjoy the world aright, till the Sea itself floweth in your veins, till you are clothed with the heavens, and crowned with the stars; and perceive yourself to be the sole heir of the whole world, and more than so, because men are in it who are every one sole heirs as well as you.' And in another place he gives us this aphorism, which contains all the truth I have been trying to express: 'It is of the nobility of man's soul that he is insatiable.'

This insatiability is only retained in the 'Estate of Innocence'. We are all born with a 'primitive and innocent clarity', which is then eclipsed by the customs and manners of men and by the evil influence of bad education. If we are to retain that primitive and innocent clarity, it must have our sympathy and encouragement long before school days and long after them. Our education begins in infancy, in the first tender relationship of mother and child; and we do not rightly encourage the values I have been speaking about unless we provide in the first and most primitive of our social groups, in the family, that respect for personality which is the foundation of liberty, and the only air or ambiance in which the personality can develop itself. The family should merge imperceptibly into the school; and then in the schools we must allow for the spontaneous emergence of groups, living and growing cells with a nucleus in some creative activity, each a field of adventure in which the grace and discipline of the individual can develop as naturally as the form and colour of a flower. This is not idealism, this is not the impracticable vision of a poet: it is biology, the basic science of life. I am speaking of facts without which our communal life cannot survive, without which all that we mean by greatness of soul, magnanimity, nobility, will die in the level deserts of a mechanized world.

The relevancy of what I have been saying to the present crisis may now begin to emerge. There still exist in the world a few small nations which have stood out against the mass neurosis of our time—that mad obsession for power and wealth which is bringing destruction to our civilization. If such nations can preserve their independent identity, then it is a situation which has great possibilities for art. I am afraid of the internationalizing tendencies of our age—of anonymous powers which would obliterate frontiers, expedite communications, standardize living. I am in favour of all that makes for diversity, variety, the reciprocity of individual units. There is a sense in which freedom implies isolation and inertia. But the real freedom is a freedom to act, to create, to move in reciprocal orbits with other free units. It is that dynamic freedom which we must seek for art, and I think we shall find it only in communities of a comfortable size, where intimacy is possible and a personality can have free scope and a friendly audience. I am not saying that a personality cannot find freedom to express itself within a vast centralized State which has the power and riches of a fifth, a fourth or one-half of the globe at its command. One might even argue that in this respect, too, there is safety in numbers. What I am saying is that a free personality, a noble soul, is independent of powers and potentates, as of all the evil and destruction they let loose in the world. But do not let us confuse spiritual freedom and personal freedom. A man may indeed possess his soul in patience, but many a noble soul has lost patience and perished miserably in a concentration camp. All that the artist demands, as a minimum, is to be let alone. He does not ask for happiness, which he knows is the rarest of the gifts of fortune. He knows, with Burckhardt, that 'only in movement, with all its pain, can life live'. But movement implies freedom, not restriction; progress rather than stability; the *relatedness* of a fraternity and the voluntary moderation of a society limited in extent, mild in power, never infringing the liberty of the person. But if power grows and liberty declines, if chaos spreads over the greater part of the world, as it does to-day, then even out of that darkness the individual can speak in his still, calm voice. And the substance of his message? From the mouth of the philosopher we call it truth, from the artist, beauty, but the poet Shelley called it love, that

The Roots of the Artist

. . . from its awful throne of patient power
In the wise heart, from the last giddy hour
Of dread endurance, from the slippery, steep,
And narrow verge of crag-like agony, springs
And folds over the world its healing wings.

II

Society and Culture

The crisis which has been developing in modern civilization ever since the advent of the Industrial Revolution has a cultural as well as an economic aspect. I realize that an attempt to dissociate these two aspects will be resisted by thoroughgoing Marxists and other materialists, but any disagreement which might thus arise would, in my opinion, be based on different conceptions of 'culture.' If culture had been always and invariably associated with civilization, as the bloom which naturally appears on a ripe peach, the Marxist might have his way without question. But one of the assumptions from which I shall start out is that culture is not a necessary and inevitable feature of a civilization—or, at least, that there is the possibility of such a qualitative difference between one culture and another that any comparison within a materialistic framework becomes meaningless. The classical example is found in Ancient Greece, where Athens and Sparta, contemporaneous as social organisms—as civilizations, that is to say—were never comparable as forcing-grounds of the creative spirit.

For nearly two centuries the great cultural tradition we inherited from the European Renaissance has been losing substance—losing substance in the literal sense of plastic concreteness. During these two centuries there has been great music, great poetry, but no great architecture—or only an exquisite diminuendo of Rococo elegancies, Classical refinements and Gothic re-creations. There have been a few great painters, but they have been individualists, without organic relationship to the social organism. The crafts have declined, the indigenous folk arts of all civilized countries have disappeared, and what we have in the place of great architecture, of architectural painting and sculpture, and of the fine crafts functionally associated with great architecture, are the mass-produced, insensitive fabrications of the machine along with its characteristic by-products—centralization, slums, social neurosis, a devitalized proletariat, a dehumanized intelligentsia.

This obvious correlation of machine production and cultural decline has produced two reactions—the Marxian one, already mentioned, which interprets that decline as one of the economic consequences of the prevailing system of production and calls for social reform, or rather for revolution, and what I will call the Ruskinian or moral reaction, which puts the blame on mechanism itself, and calls for a return to the pre-industrial system of production—or, at least, for some system that subordinates the machine to certain cultural or spiritual values.

Between Marx, who represents one school of thought, and Ruskin, who represents the other, there are a few resemblances, such as common passion for justice, but a fundamental opposition. Marx says, in effect: Let us control the machine so as to secure a just distribution of its benefits and leave culture to take care of itself; whereas Ruskin says: Put first things first—goodness, beauty, truthfulness—and you will then be compelled to abolish this evil thing, the machine, and all the social enormities which go with it.

The position I wish to take up is one which accepts the theses of both Marx and Ruskin and attempts to reconcile them. I am not going to deal specifically with either thesis, but I accept the values represented by the name of Ruskin—equally by the names of William Morris and Eric Gill—and I then ask whether there is any possibility of guiding our machine civilization towards their realization, whether, that is to say, there is any possibility of finding a place for our moral values in the world of facts which has developed inevitably from the economics of machine production.

What, in brief, are these 'facts'? They are multitudinous, and at times they seem beyond control. Machine techniques and a consequent division of labour, centralization and a cancerous growth of cities, the concentration of capital and an increasing unreality of the financial structure superimposed on these processes—these are the 'facts' of modern civilization, and however often we change the colour of our shirts or the terminology of our politics, it makes no difference to them. Some people climb up and some people climb down, but the ladder does not change, unless to become mechanized as an escalator or an elevator.

Now, though this world of facts seems immutable, all of a piece, to be accepted or rejected in its totality, I am going to suggest that this is not really so. In particular I am going to suggest that we can distinguish between what we might call 'power facts' and what we might call 'space facts,' between dynamic facts and static facts: and that once we have made this distinction, it will seem much easier to get rid of one set of facts because they are not essential, and to make up our minds to retain the other set because they are essential. Among the power facts I would include all those means which shorten or lighten labour—the machine itself, the division of labour, mass production, etc. Among the space facts I would include the location of industry and the housing of its attendant labour. The power facts are the mechanized facts, the engineering aspects of modern civilization: the space facts are the human aspects, the biological aspects, what our sociologists would call the demographic aspects.

I do not wish it to be forgotten that these two contrasted aspects of modern civilization are still within the world of facts, and that over against them is still that world of values represented by the name of Ruskin. These values are imponderable—that is why we cannot call them facts in our scientific frame of reference. But possibly these values can be reconciled with some of the facts, though not with others, and it may be that we can combine our values with a feasible selection of these facts and thus insure a civilization spontaneously productive of culture.

In this lecture I shall be content if we can get a little nearer to a definition of the contrasted terms, culture and civilization, and to an exposure of the nervous structure which connects them.

Let me begin with two significant quotations which show subtle minds exercised by this very problem. The first comes from a letter which J. B. Yeats wrote to his more famous son in July, 1917: 'I wonder whether the revolution and the creation of a Russian democracy will destroy Russian literature. I wonder also whether it was not the smallness of Athens and the minuteness of its public affairs which explains the greatness of its literature.'[1]

My second quotation occurs in an essay on 'The Man of Letters and the Future of Europe' by T. S. Eliot: 'Not the least of the effects of industrialism is that we become mechanised in mind, and consequently attempt to provide solutions in terms of *engineering*, for problems which are essentially problems of life.'[2]

Both these writers, though not professional sociologists, are asking sociological questions. Perhaps they are asking the same question. Mr. Yeats was asking whether a particular social organization

[1] *J. B. Yeats: Letters to his Son W. B. Yeats and Others*, 1869–1922, ed. by Joseph Hone (London, 1944), p. 239.

[2] *Horizon*, December 1944.

would destroy that society's literature. Mr. Eliot is asking whether we do not tend to answer such a question in the wrong terms—in mechanical terms rather than biological terms. What both writers are asserting is that there exist certain values (art, literature, spiritual freedom) which are ignored in all our plans for social betterment, and they would agree that a society which fails to establish such values is inhuman, materialistic and doomed to perish.

We are all familiar with the distinction represented by the words 'civilization' and 'culture.' Civilization, as I have already suggested, is usually thought of as in the main a materialistic achievement, culture as religious, academic and artistic; and it is then assumed that not merely a parallelism but even a causal relationship exists between the two phenomena. No view of historical realities could be more false. Indeed, almost the contrary is true, for a culture can exist without a distinctive civilization to support it (the culture of the Jews, for example); and the growth of a civilization can destroy an already existing culture, as I shall demonstrate presently.

Civilization does not need any precise definition; it is the sum total of the products and amenities of a given social organization, its wealth, customs and material achievements. It is—briefly but accurately—summed up in the phrase, a country's 'standard of living'.

The nature of culture is not so obvious. Burckhardt defined it as the sum total of those mental developments which take place spontaneously and lay no claim to universal or compulsive authority.[1] The difficulty of giving culture a definition is shown by the qualifications introduced by Burckhardt. Spontaneity, variety and freedom are all characteristics of a genuine culture, and on their account a culture can never be imposed 'ready-made' on a people —that has been one of the grosser misunderstandings of modern fascist regimes.

[1] 'Force and Freedom', *Reflections on History* (New York, 1943), p. 140.

But do not let us complicate this question by going into any deep definitions of what culture includes or implies. We know that it is expressed in certain tangible assets, among the more obvious being great literature, great music, great painting, great architecture and great sculpture. Culture may mean many other things, but no culture has been without one or more of these arts, and the greatest have had them all.

Burckhardt pointed out that the main endeavour of our contemporary civilization has been directed towards increasing the general standard of living, and 'comfort' rather than 'greatness' or even 'happiness' is the word which more nearly expresses the ideal of the modern world.

This is shown in a thousand ways. Personally I think that one of the most significant is provided by the history of the trade-union movement. Misconceived time and again by bourgeois politicians and sociologists as a political movement, it has in general (there have been exceptions among the syndicalist unions on the Continent of Europe) remained true to its early character as an organized campaign for better conditions—for better wages, fewer hours of work, better factory conditions, etc.—and along with these aggressive (but only incidentally political) functions it has always carried out functions of a purely charitable nature—sick benefits, insurance of various kinds, unemployment doles. Political action has been subsidiary to these eleemosynary aims, and the movement has remained devoid of a characteristic ideology and, indeed, of any aspirations to a cultural and political role. In Great Britain, as is well-known, it was found necessary to establish a separate body for political action, the Labour Party. The fate of this party, however, has always been dependent on the financial support of the trade unions, and its policy has been controlled by the materialistic aims of those unions.

In this respect the democratic system itself, always interpreted nowadays as majority rule, may be culturally self-stultifying. In any modern society, the people who are responsible for culture are always a minority. They constitute a separate class, designated by a special title—the intelligentsia. Even in primitive societies the artists and priests tend to be segregated as exclusive castes, sometimes on grounds as arbitrary as special birthmarks. Throughout history there are degrees of integration between such castes and society as a whole, and at some periods—the twelfth and thirteenth centuries in Europe, for example—the integration seems to be complete: every man is recognized as an artist of some sort, and the divisions in a society are by function or vocation, not by class. Nowadays the distinctions between an architect and a builder, and between a builder and a bricklayer, are class distinctions; in the Middle Ages any such distinctions were craft distinctions, the integrated grades of a single calling.

When these class distinctions exist within a democracy, a conflict at once develops between the bourgeoisie or proletariat on the one side (irrespective of their crafts) and the intelligentsia on the other side. A deep and bitter contempt or hatred for the 'highbrow' is certainly the characteristic of the democratic societies of Britain and America. Even if that conflict is of no deeper intensity than ignorance and neglect of each other's interests, it is sufficient to determine the decisive choice between culture and a higher standard of living. Burckhardt may not be right in thinking that the main endeavour of our civilization has been directed towards increasing the standards of living—that is one of the problems which I think we ought to explore—but if the choice is between culture and comfort, democracy will never vote for anything but comfort—the alternatives would never for a moment be considered seriously.

There is a certain justification for this majority attitude. 'Culture' has come to mean something quite artificial in a modern society: it is not something that springs from the people and their way of life, but something that is imposed on that way of life by education and propaganda. It is the vested interest of universities, academics, teachers, publishers and purveyors of culture in general. In these professional bodies a certain tradition of learning, a certain valuation of the arts and literatures of the past, is formulated in canons of taste, handed down as a 'tradition', and though there may be much to be said for such a tradition as a guide or a model—as a 'frame of reference'—the ordinary man is perfectly right in refusing to see that it has any relevance to his daily life. If Latin and Greek literature were to disappear, if all the architecture of the Middle Ages and the Renaissance were to be destroyed, it would not affect in the slightest the amount of butter on his bread or the warmth of the coat on his back. So why should he worry?

There is an answer to this question, but the man-in-the-street would not understand it. He would not understand it because so far his guides to knowledge, the sociologists and psychologists, the historians and politicians, have never explained in his vernacular the causes underlying the life and death of societies. For societies, like human beings, have a cycle of life. We know from our survey of the past that societies are subject to the alternation of two moods which we might call *zest* and *apathy*. Zest in life is marked by adventure, by expression and creative activity in the arts; apathy, which may be accompanied by material wealth and vast possessions, implies first security, then boredom, and finally decadence. Societies are sometimes overwhelmed by superior force; but more often, like old soldiers, they simply fade away. We are all familiar with the case of the successful business man who retires from work apparently in good health and with the expectation of ten or twenty years of secure enjoyment of the good things of life; he often dies within a year or two for no explicable reason. He dies of boredom. There was a similar phenomenon in the Middle Ages, before successful business men had been evolved by a commercial civilization. Monks who retired into monasteries were attacked by a fatal disease of the will which was called *accidie*:[1] again, it was inanition or boredom, an affliction due to security, seclusion, absence of adventure and struggle.

Burckhardt, and many other philosophers of history, considering these facts, have come to the conclusion that war has a vital function in social development. 'Lasting peace,' wrote Burckhardt, 'not only leads to enervation; it permits the rise of a mass of precarious, fear-ridden, distressful lives which would not have survived without it and which nevertheless clamour for their "rights," cling somehow to existence, bar the way to genuine ability, thicken the air and as a whole degrade the nation's blood. War restores real ability to honour.'

This point of view ignores the fact that it is the brave and the strong who perish first in war: that it is the maimed and afflicted who then inherit the earth. War exhausts a society and, if prolonged, bleeds it to death. This is now more obvious than it was in Burckhardt's day (he was writing about 1870); modern war is total in scope and annihilating in effect.

Realizing this truth, other philosophers have sought for a 'moral equivalent of war'. This was the title of a famous essay by William James, who argued that society should seek and would find the moral equivalent of war in such dangerous occupations as mountaineering, exploration, coal-mining, and generally in fighting nature rather than other societies.

On the other hand, a quantity of evidence—biological, historical and sociological—can be brought together (it was done with great effect by Kropotkin in *Mutual Aid*) to show that societies only cohere by virtue of a natural principle of co-operation. Much evidence of a psychological nature has been accumulated in recent years which proves that war and conflict, as well as individual

[1] Cf. Chaucer, *Canterbury Tales*, 'The Persones Tale'.

neuroses, are regressions from a natural condition of interdependence. War is a disease of society just as schizophrenia is a disease of the human personality, and society can only be cured of its ills by returning to its 'biological heritage of co-operation and true social integration.'[1]

If we accept this hypothesis of social behaviour—and I do not see that any other hypothesis is possible if we are to retain any belief in the worth of life—then the sociological problem is reduced to this: how, within a society based on the natural principle of mutual aid, can we maintain zest in life?

We have seen that security and passiveness are deleterious, destroying the will to life. We need a principle of strife or rivalry which is not mutually destructive, or destructive of the material structure of civilization, but which nevertheless gives the moral equivalent, the *courageous tone* of war.

There is no doubt in my mind that this principle is found in the pursuit of cultural aims. The question then becomes: what form of society will best incite its citizens to that pursuit? It is a vital question, which sociologists and psychologists ought to be able to answer: there is the whole history of the world in evidence.

I would like to suggest that the answer is contained within Burckhardt's definition of culture. Burckhardt saw the decisive quality of a culture in its *spontaneity*, and further suggested that a culture could lay no claim to universal or compulsive authority. 'Culture is that millionfold process by which the spontaneous, unthinking activity of a race is transformed into considered action, or indeed, at its last and highest stage, in science and especially philosophy, into pure thought.'[2]

[1] Cf. William Galt, 'The Principle of Co-operation in Behaviour,' *Quarterly Review of Biology*, Vol. XV, No. 4, Dec. 1940, pp. 401–10. Also Trigant Burrow, *Biology of Human Conflict* (New York, 1937).

[2] *Op. cit.*, p. 158.

Spontaneity is not an inexplicable and mystical phenomenon. But it does imply an absence of conscious determination. It is action which results from the unexpected collision or collocation of diverse elements. If a lighted match comes into contact with gunpowder the result is an explosion, which is spontaneous enough. If certain physical or chemical changes take place within an inflammable substance, the result is 'spontaneous' combustion. Similarly, spontaneity in the cultural development of a society depends on the free circulation of a great number and diversity of cultural elements, i.e., ideas, images, forms. These meet in the minds of sensitive men, and we call the result 'inspiration'—it is spontaneous combustion on the mental plane. It was for this reason that Milton in his *Areopagitica* argued so eloquently for the free circulation of the printed word—he realized that the vitality of thought depended on its uncontrolled diffusion; and the fact that schism and heresies are thereby let loose is no argument against such philosophic freedom, for only in that manner can they be brought out into the open and defeated. Truth and virtue would emerge all the stronger from the clash.

Variety and freedom may seem obvious enough as prerequisites of cultural vitality, but they imply a third element which is not at all obvious but which is nevertheless the most essential of all. Burckhardt does not specifically mention it in his definition of culture (which comes from his *Reflections on History*) but it is explicit enough in his great work on the *Civilization of the Renaissance in Italy*. It is a question of size. Culture, as J. B. Yeats remarks in the letter I have quoted, is somehow related to smallness and minuteness. The greatest achievements in architecture, painting and literature are linked with relatively very small communities, city-states like Athens, Florence, Siena. This is the complicated question which I hope to investigate more closely in my next lecture, but if we reverse the statement we can say without fear of contradiction that there is no historical evidence which in any way connects the *quality* of culture with the *magnitude* of states. All the evidence, at a first glance, suggests that quality is associated in some way with limitations of size.

I believe that in this question of social size we have the key to the problem of social zest. There is no obvious zest, no principle or cause of rivalry, in a condition of mere uniformity. The bigger a state, the more closely organized its all-over aspect, the more average its constituent units, the less chance for the development of variety or diversity.

Size, as a matter of fact, has a biological limit. A state may get so big that pieces begin to break off. There is a limit to the amount of space and the number of people that can be controlled from a centre. The British Commonwealth and the Union of Socialist Soviet Republics have both shown tendencies to dissociation and fragmentation—expressed in a wise policy of devolution. When such a process of devolution sets in, the role of culture as a binding element becomes very important.

One of the tasks awaiting sociology is to discover the principles which should govern such processes of devolution. What is the optimum size for a unit of government? Under what social conditions is culture likely to arise spontaneously and to be pursued with zest? What features in modern industrial society militate against each such cultural vitality? How can it be fostered by education? What is the effect of such agents of diffusion as the press, the radio, and the cinema?

But, as Mr. Eliot says, it is in the terms of *life*, and not of *mechanics*, that these questions must be answered. Culture is fundamentally a biological phenomenon: we use the same word 'culture' for bacteria and for works of art, and that is absolutely right. The conditions under which a culture of art will germinate are to be determined as precisely and as scientifically as the conditions which determine a culture of penicillin in the laboratory. But the process itself is vital, is spontaneous, is a *generation* of new forms of life. The wider life of society depends on the generation of this molecular life, and unless we provide the social conditions under which the molecular processes of culture can take place, our whole civilization is doomed to pass away without leaving a trace.

The basic requirements seem to me to be four in number:

1. *The reconstruction of our physical environment to secure the most favourable framework for a vital culture.*
2. *A social system without wide diversity of personal wealth.*
3. *An industrial system that gives the worker a direct responsibility for the quality of his work.*
4. *An educational system that preserves and matures the innate aesthetic sensibility of man.*

These four requirements together constitute a revolution far more extreme than any usually envisaged by politicians. They imply not merely a new social order, but a new way of life, a new trend of civilization. I shall submit these requirements to a more detailed examination in subsequent lectures; for the moment I would merely like to establish for them a reasonable degree of practicability.

By practicability I do not mean the theoretical possibility of planning the necessary structures, but rather the degree in which social pressures can be created which will lead to the spontaneous expression of good taste—those imponderable elements of style and integrity which are the mark of a great epoch in art. It might be possible to plan, say, a neo-classical style, and impose it on the people by drastic rebuilding, by re-education and central direction; but a great period of artistic creation is never planned; it grows out of the grass roots of a civilization and is largely unconscious in its origins and development. Its fundamental character is derived from a certain *instinct for form* which is diffused among the whole people.

If we bear this fact in mind we may avoid easy rational solutions for what is essentially an irrational problem.

For that reason any grandiose schemes for rebuilding our monstrous cities, for replanning the countryside, redistributing populations and industries—all these will have but a negative effect on the general standard of taste unless accompanied by the rebirth of a basic or native aesthetic sensibility. We are already familiar with the problems which arise when people are moved from slums to decent housing estates. There are two alternatives: either you allow people to move in with all their cheap furniture, their hideous possessions of all sorts, and thereby destroy the most potent because the most intimate aspect of environmental influence; or you furnish the new homes before the people move in—you provide a ready-made environment which has no sense of familiarity, which the people will resent, and which they will gradually pervert. Such people should bring with them a desire—a natural longing—for an interior environment which is aesthetically in keeping with the architectural setting. If they had such a longing, they would have an aesthetic appreciation of the architecture itself, and it would be they, the people, who would demand, and whose demand would create, a style of architecture.

Our examination of this first requirement therefore throws us back on the problem of sensibility.

As for the second requirement—a social system without wide diversity of personal wealth—this may seem of doubtful urgency. The style of the Renaissance, it may be argued, was created by a society which tolerated extremes of wealth, and even the glory of Greece was based on slavery. I shall have something to say about the significance of the social hierarchy in my next lecture, and for the moment I would merely point out that we who live in the machine age live under conditions which are fundamentally different from any in the past, and in this respect we must not feel bound by historical precedents. To mention one difference: the machine is *our* slave, and the problem is no longer who is to do the work, but how are the products of the machine to be distributed without creating economic chaos. It is a problem we have not yet solved. But, obviously, the machine produces on a mass scale, and it must have a mass of consumers. The machine is not aristocratic: it does not respond to social or financial bribes. It will do its best for the biggest market. The widest diffusion of riches is the economy which will encourage quality in machine production. Machine products are cheap and nasty now, because there are millions of poor people. Abolish poverty, and the whole qualitative aspect of machine production would be transformed.

But I am speaking as if machines were conscious agents, and that brings me to the third requirement I mentioned: an industrial system which gives the worker a direct responsibility for his work—an old story, you may think, and you will again be prepared to hear the names of Ruskin, Morris and Eric Gill. An old story, but a true story, and not one that has been made obsolete by modern developments in machine production. The machine must be given a conscience, and we do not give it a conscience merely by allowing it to re-act mechanically to the financial stimulus of this or that market. There must be what T. E. Hulme in another connection called 'a critique of satisfaction'[1]—that is to say, the object manufactured should satisfy, not merely a need, but also a standard of perfection. The need is functional, and the degree in which the manufactured object satisfies that need can be measured by mechanical standards; but perfection can only be measured by a human intuition of an absolute quality.

Once again we are back at an imponderable element: we may now call it intuition rather than sensibility, but essentially it is

[1] *Speculations*, ed. by Herbert Read (London and New York, 2nd ed., 1936), pp. 12–23.

something human and personal, something innate. Unless that human assessment is introduced into the process of production, we cannot have any final sense of, any reaching after, perfection; and without that we cannot have any practical education of the sensibilities. Education, which is the final requirement, is not, as I shall venture to assert, a question of receiving instruction at a particular stage of life: it is the constant reaction of the human senses to material needs with a progressive sense of economy and skill. I believe that somewhere in this direction lies the whole secret of taste or sensibility. Good taste may be exuberant, but even when most exuberant—as, for example, in certain types of Rococo ornament—it abates nothing of skill in the act of creation. But what, then, is skill?

The word is derived from a root which means to separate or divide, and its original meaning was near to 'discrimination' or 'discernment'. The history of the word suggests that the process of perception is somehow involved in skill, and that happens also to be the latest conclusion of psychology. I am faced now with the difficulty of expressing in a simple sentence or two the main outlines of a whole theory of perception and learning. This is the Gestalt hypothesis, which is the basis of a distinct school of psychology, and it is very relevant to our discussion. The Gestalt psychologist says that skill is the product of discrimination, that discrimination is made possible by the felt difference between one action and another, and that the difference which is thus felt is one of economy or grace. What is most economical in an action is also the most rhythmical or graceful; and it is the aesthetic perception of this difference, at a very primitive level, which determines the whole process of learning how to do a thing skilfully. And perception, the Gestalt psychologist argues, has a natural bias towards forms that are aesthetically satisfying.

This discovery—not so much a discovery as a psychological

explanation of truths as old as mankind—has a profound significance for the whole theory of education, and I shall devote a separate lecture to it. For the moment it is sufficient to note that the discovery implies, not merely that education should be aesthetic, but even that education, in so far as it is the acquisition of skill, of grace, of efficient action, *is* aesthetic; and that any other method of education is merely learning a bad habit—a clumsy way of doing anything.

It follows from this theory that taste, as a generalized phenomenon, depends entirely on the effective teaching of various skills. *A people of taste, or a period of taste, is always one in which there exists a system of education or upbringing based on the acquisition of integrated physical skills.* There you have my main generalization, the substance of all I have to say on this or any related subject. It is a generalization which I am convinced can be substantiated, not only by psychological experiment, but also by the whole evidence of history. Wherever you have a people that possesses infallible taste, there you will find that the principle of education or the merely instinctive mode of upbringing is based on the acquisition of physical skills—skills which may be either practical and utilitarian, or ritualistic and recreational, but which always involve, as the price of efficiency, the cultivation of harmony and grace.

This seems to me to be so obvious a truth that it is difficult to select an illustration which will not seem trite. Peasant art, for example, is invariably in good taste; and it is the art of a people whose education is essentially manual. The art is in the skill with which the objects are made: there is no conscious division between form and purpose. The art of most savage peoples is essentially peasant art with these same characteristics, but the characteristics belong to the art and are instilled by a method of upbringing, a social organization, which is not necessarily primitive or savage. The same characteristics are found in an 'uncivilized' but nevertheless highly refined and even sophisticated people such as the Balinese. Miguel Covarrubias, an artist who has lived among these people and noticed their ways with the eye of an artist, tells us that 'Balinese art is not in the class of the "great" arts like Chinese painting—the conscious production of works of art for their own sake, with an aesthetic value apart from their function. Again, it is too refined, too developed, to fit into peasant arts, nor is it one of the primitive arts, those subject to ritual and tribal laws, which we call "primitive" because their aesthetics do not conform to ours. Their art is a highly-developed, although informal Baroque folk-art that combines the peasant liveliness with the refinement of the classicism of Hinduistic Java, but free of conservative prejudice and with a new vitality fired by the exuberance of the demoniac spirit of the tropical primitive'.[1] Mr. Covarrubias also tells us that the art of the Balinese is anonymous, the expression of collective thought. He also tells us that there are no words in the Balinese language for 'art' and 'artist'—'making a beautiful offering, and carving a stone temple gate, and making a set of masks are tasks of equal aesthetic importance, and although the artist is regarded as a preferred member of the community, there is no separate class of artists, and a sculptor is simply a 'carver' or a figure-maker, and the painter a picture-maker'. 'Everybody in Bali seems to be an artist, coolies and princes, priests and peasants, men and women alike, can dance, play musical instruments, paint, or carve in wood or stone. It was often surprising to discover that an otherwise poor and dilapidated village harboured an elaborate temple, a great orchestra, or a group of actors of repute.' There are many other significant features of this civilization which have a bearing on our subject and which this perceptive artist notes, for example, 'the important factor of leisure resulting from well-organized agricultural co-operatism', and 'the fact that the Balinese did not per-

[1] Miguel Covarrubias, *Island of Bali* (New York and London, 1937), p. 165.

mit the centralization of the artistic knowledge in a special intellectual class'. But the most important fact of all is that their system of education implies that everyone, from prince to peasant, should learn the crafts of painting, wood-carving, music, and the making of musical instruments, to dance and to sing, just as naturally as they learn every other craft. Education is a craft, craft is education, and as a result 'a commoner may be as finished an artist as the educated nobleman, although he may be an agriculturalist, a tradesman, or even a coolie'. Taste, that is to say, is not the standard of a class or an educated minority: it is the possession of a people.

Let us turn finally to the evidence offered by the oldest surviving, the most persistent and aesthetically the most perfect civilization known to the world—the Chinese. Chinese taste has degenerated during the past two centuries, perhaps as a result of its contacts with the Western Hemisphere, but as a continuous phenomenon it has survived the artistic epochs of Greece and Rome, of the Middle Ages and of the European Renaissance and its vagaries, and even to-day shows signs of a vitality not yet exhausted. At the base of all this plastic civilization, this endless epoch of prevailing good taste, is the manual craft of calligraphy, or brush-writing.[1] 'In China,' writes Chiang Yee, 'calligraphy is the

[1] Cf. William Bowyer Honey, *The Ceramic Art of China* (London, 1945), pp. 3–4: 'Chinese art and literature have flowered continually into that mysterious creative synthesis of form and colour, association and allusion, which we call poetry. There mere brush-writing is itself poetical, aspiring to give life and rhythm and meaning to every stroke, while painting is for the Chinese always a branch of calligraphy, with the same ideal of vitality and expressiveness in brushwork. Painting for them is never the glorification of man, but rests on an almost mystical belief in the wonder and significance of all objects of sense alike. In Chinese works of art we are aware of a poetical sensuousness delighting in shape and substance, whether in a tree or a mountain, a written character, a pottery bowl, a worn jade ornament or a patinated

most popular of the arts. It is a national taste, a common aesthetic instinct nourished in every Chinese from childhood up. Anything which can claim to be a work of art has some connection, obvious or subtle, with calligraphy.'[1] From the beginning of their education, Chinese children devote at least one hour a day to this craft, and their practice of it never ceases; it continues as a natural occupation long after their schooldays. Another Chinese writer, Lin Yutang, tells us that 'so fundamental is the place of calligraphy in Chinese art *as a study of form and rhythm in the abstract* that we may say it has provided the Chinese people with a basic aesthetics, and it is through calligraphy that the Chinese have learned their basic notions of line and form. It is therefore impossible to talk about Chinese art without understanding Chinese calligraphy and its artistic inspiration. There is, for instance, not one type of Chinese architecture, whether it be the *pailou*, the pavilion or the temple, whose sense of harmony and form is not directly derived from certain types of Chinese calligraphy.' [2] (Fig. 18.)

I do not quote these examples to explain the secret of Chinese art, or of art generally. The basic unity of art, from calligraphy to architecture, may be recognized, but what has this to do with the personal possession of taste? We lack the faculties to appreciate, let alone create, the basic unity of art, and how shall we acquire them? Surely it is obvious that in taste, no less than in the creation of works of art, the aesthetic faculty itself is involved, and that only in so far as we feel balance and symmetry, proportion and rhythm,

bronze, stressing always, with a half-melancholy resignation, whatever is enduring in them. In short, we are aware of a refinement and cultivation of the pleasures of the senses, a care for disinterested contemplation, and a delight in the exercise of the mind, which all speak of a people more truly civilized than ourselves.' (Figs. 20*a*, *b*.)

[1] Chiang Yee, *Chinese Calligraphy* (London, 1938), p. 17.

[2] Lin Yutang, *My Country and My People* (New York, 1935), p. 291.

naturally and instinctively in all the acts of our daily life, may we claim to possess taste. But, once we admit this, we can see the tragic deprivations which are involved in our *actual* way of life. We simply have no *normal* aesthetic experiences. They are completely lacking from the routine occupations of a mechanized civilization—not only from the daily lives of the machine-tenders and the distributors of machine-made goods, but still more drastically from the wan existences of clerks and intellectuals. And that, we have to recognize, is part of the price we pay for the comforts of civilization—for the motor-cars and refrigerators, the canned food and the nylon stockings. But why should we aggravate these evils by a system of education and upbringing divorced from all that is vital and sensuous? Should we not rather attempt to compensate for the unnaturalness of a machine civilization by the most extensive use of all those forms of education and enjoyment that engage the senses in a progressive cultivation of skill and grace? Such is the common sense of the situation. A standard of taste will never emerge from people who from birth are bound and blinkered, whose muscles never learn to move in rhythm, whose senses never learn to discriminate between one formal arrangement and another. Aesthetically speaking, the modern child's development is arrested at the cocoon stage: it never spreads its wings in the sunlight, never dazzles the world with colour and movement.

At the same time, it is salutary to remember that a people can possess taste without the aids of education in our sense of the word. The Balinese are innocent of college entrance examinations and I.Q. tests. A country can also preserve its standards of taste and yet be, like China, a land of scholars. A good scholar, in China, would almost certainly be a good calligrapher and even a good painter. It is not education that matters, if by education we mean the acquisition of knowledge, the learning of principles and precepts, and those alone. What matters is a certain integrity of development in the individual so that his mind is never cultivated at the expense of his senses, or his senses at the expense of his mind. There are plenty of people in our industrial civilization who learn a mechanical skill, but it is not an integrated skill: it is not geared in any way to the rest of their mental faculties, nor to the rest of their social activities. It is, and remains, an isolated habit, learned at the end of the educational process instead of being the educational process itself. Skill should be taught as a basic education of the senses, from infancy. Our particular trouble, in this 'air-conditioned nightmare' which we call a civilization, is that we have lost the very notion of cultivating the senses, until butter-fingered and tongue-tied, half-blind and deaf to all nervous vibrations, we stumble through life unaware of its most appealing aspects, lost to its intensest joys and communions. Frustrated and brutalized, we drift between the boredom of peace and the self-inflicted wounds of war, and dismiss as lunatic those few quiet voices that speak of love and beauty and of the renunciations we must accept, of power, wealth and pride, if we would have the influence of beauty and love prevail in our lives.

III

The Social Basis of Great Architecture

Architecture is an art—the art of building. It is not merely building as a functional activity of human beings—it is the products of that activity in so far as they reach a certain standard of excellence which we call art.

Associated with architecture are other arts, the most important being the art of town-planning, which is perhaps not so much an art as a science. Now it is obvious that in so far as building and planning are a response to human needs, to that extent they have a social basis. To show the relation between the social pattern and the town plan is a task which we can safely leave to the sociologist. What I am going to attempt to demonstrate in this lecture is that building in so far as it is architecture—that is to say, in so far as it is an art—also depends on the social pattern. Venturing still further, I am going to suggest that the very quality of the architecture—its aesthetic value or integrity—is directly related to a particular kind of social pattern. Some societies produce great architecture, others produce architecture which is only a dim reflection of past epochs of greatness, still others produce no architecture at all. What is the secret of *great* architecture?

The Social Basis of Great Architecture

The subject seems to invite a shower of easy commonplaces. Architecture is, of course, primarily building, and building must be functional. But everything, in such a categorical imperative, will depend on the nature of the function. If, for example, we adopt Le Corbusier's intransigent definition of a house as 'a machine to live in', and then with this definition in mind turn to the critical examination of typical Baroque houses, it would at first seem but logical to condemn them as arbitrary and irresponsible examples of non-functional building. But the Baroque architect would accept the challenge implied in this modern definition of a house. Sir John Vanbrugh, to take the most abstract and therefore the most extreme of English Baroque architects, once defined the qualities he aimed at in his houses as 'State, Beauty and Convenience,' in that order. Beauty and Convenience we accept: we even tend to identify them; but what is this third quality—State—which is even given first place? At once we are up against a sociological factor, for 'State' in Vanbrugh's time was the quality of a certain manner of living: the manner of the typical oligarchs of the seventeenth and eighteenth centuries. In building a house for the Earl of Carlisle or the Duke of Marlborough, Vanbrugh would have been neglecting the strict functional requirements of his task if he had been any less extravagant and, in our eyes, irresponsible. Indeed, Vanbrugh himself claimed that his houses were the most convenient ever yet planned. And they are in fact a series of separate, and yet interdependent, suites, so organized that the owner of the house and his principal guests could live and hold their levees independently, and yet all meet, for more stately occasions, in the Great Hall. As Geoffrey Webb has pointed out, 'this is not unreasonable'. 'In his plans this peculiar method of internal arrangement is worked out most conscientiously and logically, great care being taken, almost invariably, to provide a way out of each suite independently of the others, and without the necessity of passing through the anteroom. It is quite clear that the planning is specially adapted to a special type of daily life, quite as carefully as the most up-to-date modern villa residence is moulded on the requirements of the social and intimate life of the middle-class household that will inhabit it.'[1]

So after all, Castle Howard and Blenheim (Fig. 5) were designed as machines to live in: their design was determined by the special function they had to perform. A very short analysis of Baroque architecture has thus revealed what we may dismiss as merely one of the commonplaces of our subject. It does not need the science of sociology to discover that the size, extent and ground-plan of a building are dependent on the domestic or social purposes which it has to serve. A knowledge of social customs and national habits is a very useful aid to the appreciation of architecture, but nothing more. It will never, for example, explain the difference between good architecture and bad architecture.

A most superficial analysis will yield a whole class of materialistic factors which must be dismissed as of little significance in this connection, though they may have a very marked influence on architectural design. These may be classified as geographical and economic, though in the end they are perhaps only economic. If an American millionaire wants to build a house of Cotswold stone in Florida, there is nothing to prevent him doing so. But a farmer in Kent or Kentucky cannot build his house of stone of any kind because he cannot afford the cost of transport: he must use brick or weather-boarding. But the cross-influences of regional materials, economic scarcity and functional requirements produce some very definite stylistic modifications which often puzzle the layman, and for that reason a short digression from my main argument may be justified.

[1] *The Complete Works of Sir John Vanbrugh*, Vol. IV (The Letters), ed. by Geoffrey Webb (London, 1928), p. xvii.

Let us begin, for example, with a simple contrast in domestic habits. The Englishman, to the mystification of all foreigners, likes to sit in front of an open fire, his feet and face roasted, his back exposed to a more or less icy hinterland. Our Continental friends, on the other hand, have what seems to us the embarrassing habit of sitting round a table in the middle of the room, neither too hot nor too cold, but condemned to contemplate, instead of the inspiring flicker of the firelight, the all-too-human features of the person sitting opposite. No doubt many curious national characteristics can be traced to this difference in national habits, but let us trace their effects on domestic architecture.

An open fire is a dangerous area. It must be so constructed that there is no risk of the heat and flames setting fire to the house. This means in effect a substantial chimney-breast and stack, built of brick or stone. If cost is no object and materials are plentiful, you can protect your fires wherever convenience dictates that they should be situated. But in most cases materials will be scarce or the cost of them an important consideration. The result is that the English and early 'Colonial' house tends to be built round its chimney. If you can only afford the material for one chimney-stack, then the rooms are grouped round it in a primitive wigwam formation, and we have even hit upon the expedient of building two or more houses round the one chimney-stack, which results in that peculiarly hideous and peculiarly English monstrosity—the semi-detached villa, which might be called wigwam for two or more families. If you can afford brick or stone for the outer walls of your house, then the chimney-stacks are embodied in these outer walls, usually at the gable ends, and you thus get the characteristic English farmhouse and cottage. It is only when you can afford brick or stone for all your walls, interior as well as exterior, that the architect can design the house with freedom. Even then, in the English house he will have the problem of accommodating his chimneys. The chimney plays a great part in the design of the English house (Fig. 1), and becomes an obsession in the case of an architect like Sir Edwin Lutyens. It is all due to our pleasant but irrational habit of sitting round the fire.

But if, as in Austria and Germany, houses are heated by slow-combustion stoves, which are provided with their own pottery insulation and only need a pipe or vent for exhaust; or if, as in Italy and other Mediterranean countries, the rigours of a short winter are endured with nothing more than a charcoal brazier under the table, then chimneys are no longer a serious consideration. It is true that there may be other difficulties which are complications of an equally exasperating kind, such as excessive heat and glaring light; but I have taken the fireside as merely a typical social convention which has a decisive effect, not only on the planning of the house, but also on the structural appearance. The final and most decisive effect of all comes with the introduction of central-heating and air-conditioning. The plan of the house is then completely liberated from the vertical axis of the chimney-stack, and the architect is given a new horizontal freedom of which he does not hesitate to take full advantage (Fig. 2).

Such structural revolutions do not make the difference between good architecture and bad architecture. They merely give the architect certain elements which he has to accommodate in his design. The design itself, as an aesthetic value, will be determined by quite different considerations.

One more example of this interaction of social factors and structural requirements may be noted—the evolution of the Gothic church window. It will lead us a little nearer to the heart of the subject. The original purpose of a window was, of course, to let in light, but because of the difficulty of heating the churches, and for structural reasons which I need not enlarge on, the windows were deep-set and narrow—for that reason we call them lancet windows. Meanwhile, in the ninth or tenth century, the art of stained glass painting had been discovered, and the windows were gradually widened to accommodate the translucent pictures. The architect was set an increasingly difficult problem, but in the course of the next three or four centuries he solved it, in a manner which still evokes our wonder and admiration. Onwards from the thirteenth century, as a result of that revolution in sentiment which we call the Franciscan Movement, an ever more pictorial and naturalistic treatment was demanded of the glass painters, and the churches and cathedrals became something analogous to the movies of to-day—that is to say, spectacles for the visual entertainment and education of the illiterate masses. The windows were thus put under an even greater strain, and in the course of the fourteenth century those styles were evolved which in England we call Decorated and Perpendicular, and which were primarily determined by the demand for window space. Incidentally, now that he was required to work on such a grandiose scale, the glass painter found that he had to alter his whole conception of design and tonality. The windows, as they became wider and higher and more intricate, demanded of the stained glass painter an effect that was not too heavy for the expanse to be filled, nor too clumsy for its delicacy. But this is a secondary effect. The primary effect is in the design of the window aperture and its supporting tracery. The English Perpendicular window, as we often find it to-day, devoid of its original glass paintings, is a curious affair, and yet its *raison d'être*, or functional necessity, was so strong, that the rest of the architectural structure had to be adapted to it (Fig. 4). Perpendicular architecture is to a considerable extent to be interpreted as an eleborate framework for the coloured pictures with which the windows were originally filled. The whole of this development was due to sociological factors: to the growth of naturalistic sentiment within the Christian religion, and the consequent strong desire to visualize the life of

Christ and of the Christian saints for the benefit of the great mass of people who could not read the Vulgate, nor even the popularized versions in vernacular such as the Golden Legend. This development could not, of course, have taken place without a progressive improvement in building technique and the various subsidiary crafts. But I think we may assert that the primary factor was, in the strictest sense of the word, sociological. A stylistic change in architecture was due to the impact of a widely diffused longing, a collective sentiment which demanded, not exactly expression, but at any rate satisfaction.

But we have not yet reached the heart of our subject. The architectural response is still the solution of a practical problem, and I do not think we can state our problem until we have eliminated the functional element and can ask whether the architecture is in any sense determined by the collective consciousness of society—or, as we might say, by spiritual factors. The question I am going to ask is this: Are there elements in the aesthetic characteristics of architecture which can be correlated with collective social phenomena, so that we can say, for example, that the greatness of one particular period of architecture—its significant form and beauty—is due to the existence of special qualities in a whole people or nation?

I have at various points introduced the words 'great' or 'greatness', and in doing so I have assumed the existence of, and intention to apply, a certain standard of 'values'. It will, in fact, be found that I assume the peculiar greatness of two epochs of architecture—Greek architecture in its full Doric purity and strength, and Gothic architecture in its most daring and exalted spirituality. These epochs I place on a higher level than, say, Romanesque or Baroque, simply because they achieve that unique synthesis which we call 'originality,' whereas the other periods I have mentioned are in some degree derivative. I will not attempt to defend this criterion on this occasion—it is possibly a task which would need very considerable support of a somewhat metaphysical kind. But I believe that it represents a certain consensus of opinion: the devotees of Baroque, for example, always suffer from their consciousness of defending a lost cause.

This apology made, let me return to the main question: To what special qualities, if any, in a people or a society, is the greatness of their architecture due?

It is a big question, and one not without its relevance to the ideological conflict which has been dividing the world for the past forty years or more. Here, for example, is a thesis which I would first ask you to consider without the prejudice which the name of the author might provoke:

'The proof of the endowment of a true artist is always to be found in the fact that his work of art expressed the general will of a period. Perhaps that is most clearly shown in architecture. . . . The religious mystical world of the Christian Middle Ages, turning inwards upon itself, found forms of expression which were possible only for that world—for that world alone could they be of service. A Gothic stadium is as unthinkable as a Romanesque railway station or a Byzantine market-hall. The way in which the artist of the Middle Ages, of the beginnings of the modern world, found the artistic solution for the buildings which he was commissioned to create is in the highest degree striking and admirable. That way, however, is no evidence that the conception of the content of life held by the folk of his day was in itself either absolutely right or absolutely wrong; it is evidence only that works of art have rightly mirrored the inner mind of a past age. . . .'[1]

That, I think we must admit, is a respectacle theory, worthy of our serious consideration; the words come from a speech of

[1] *Hitler's Speeches*, trans. by Norman H. Baynes (Oxford, 1942), Vol. I, pp. 394–5, Speech at Nuremberg, 6 September 1938.

Hitler's. The idea is not his own: it is shared by many students of the Middle Ages. The assertion is that the architects of the Gothic period did express in their work what Hitler calls 'the general will of the period'. They mirrored 'the inner mind' of their age; they expressed a certain conception of life held collectively by the people of their time.

It is very significant that already in the passage I have quoted, Hitler questions the value, or shall we say the truth, of the particular conception of life held by the medieval people. There is no evidence, he says, to show that such a conception was absolutely right or wrong: what we should admire is merely the fact that, right or wrong, a collective conception was embodied in the art of the period. And he goes on, in this same speech, to make perfectly clear that it is not his conception of life. It is quite conceivable, he admits, that in the religious sphere people will always hark back to the form language of a period in which Christianity in its view of the world appeared to meet every need. But he himself definitely replaces the concept of religion with the concept of *race*, which he describes as determining the new view of the world; and for a model for the artistic expression of this particular concept he returns, not to the Middle Ages, but to an age which possessed a racial rather than a religious conception of life, namely, to Ancient Rome, to 'the evidences and memories of that mighty imperial Power of antiquity which, although in fact destroyed fifteen hundred years ago, still as an ideal force lives on and works on in the imaginations of men. . . .'

It is said that Hitler composed his own speeches, and certainly their style suggests it. But he was briefed by a competent intelligence service, even in these questions of art and culture. It may be that the particular view he was expressing in the speech from which I have quoted has had a very general currency among German art historians, but his words seemed to strike a familiar chord in my memory, and on looking through my notes I found the clue. It was in the work of a fellow Austrian (and one who welcomed the Nazi regime when it came), Josef Strzygowski. It is quite conceivable that Hitler had at some time read some of the voluminous writings of this art historian—they were famous enough thirty years ago.

I think some of Strzygowski's researches were extremely valuable: he succeeded, more definitely than any of his predecessors, in separating the Northern and the Southern, the specifically Gothic and the specifically Classical elements, in Christian art. But on the top of this purely stylistic analysis he elaborated a theory which I will give you in his own words (or rather, those of his English translator):

'The origin of Christian Church art is much more definitely interlinked with geographical, racial and national characters than people have hitherto been led to suppose; they have under-estimated the importance of the list of peoples mentioned in the Acts of the Apostles as present in Jerusalem at the First Pentecost. Spiritual movements are superficial in comparison with the fixity of geographical factors; they may modify this or that, embrace foreign influences, and even end by losing their identity; but they can never produce new or decisive values.'[1]

To make it quite clear what this theory means, here is another quotation from the same source:

'Just as there was never a single and uniform Christianity, so from the very first there was never a single stem, far less a single root, from which Christian art sprang. On the contrary, the time when there was still no uniformity in the Church and still no Christian State was precisely that when the controlling factor was the national spirit, which varied from one people to another

[1] *Origin of Christian Church Art*, trans. by O. M. Dalton and H. J. Braunholtz (Oxford, 1923), pp. 185–6.

According to the received idea, Christian art rose as a homogeneous growth from Hellenistic and imperial Roman ground. We have seen that these limits must be extended. The moment the geographical horizon is widened, the vital and creative force is discovered in local genius. Race, nationality, and economic condition count beyond question far more than political and intellectual connections.'[1]

It will be seen that Strzygowski is more positive than Hitler. Hitler does admit that spiritual movements, such as the Christian religion in the Middle Ages, may find expression in art, and especially in architecture. But for Strzygowski it is all *Blut und Boden*, blood and soil: the local genius of the rooted and localized race, sustained in some mysterious way by an almost chemical process of symbiosis. Hitler favoured this hypothesis, thought it was the specifically modern hypothesis destined to receive one more manifestation in the culture of the Dritte Reich. But on to the materialistic hypothesis of the art historian he grafted an ideological doctrine.

It is not part of my intention to refute either the historian's hypothesis or the politician's doctrine. My own theory is more inclusive: art can express anything. And it can express nothing. It can express blood and soil, race and religion, and merely the practical functions of industrial activity. And equally all these things can get along quite well without art. I am not sure that the Jews are a race according to Hitler's definition of the term, but certainly there is a Jewish conception of life; no religious community has such a long tradition of integral spiritual vitality; and yet neither the race nor the religion has found expression in a specific architecture. I know there are synagogues—in the Near East and in Southern Spain—of great beauty, but they are mostly the work of Arab craftsmen, and their form language is abstract rather than religious. The Russians

[1] *Op. cit.*, p. 30.

are another race without a characteristic form language—their architecture is eclectic—a mingling of Oriental and Byzantine styles until modern times, and in modern times it is quite characterless. One could multiply such negative examples from both the ancient and the modern world until even a Strzygowski would have to admit that there is no *inevitable* connection between geographical and racial factors and creative genius in art. The mesh of that particular net, in my opinion, is much too wide.

We must seek for some alternative explanation of the possible interaction of the collective will and the forms of art. Since it is evident that this collective will, whether it is of a racial, a national or a religious character, may or may not find expression in art, we must seek for an explanation of an incidental, even of an accidental, nature. What is not inevitable must to some extent be arbitrary. We might even find that arbitrariness is of the essence of the explanation, for I know of no recorded instance of a race, or a creed, that by taking thought was able to create for itself an appropriate art form. There may be a will to power, a will to many intentional states of mind, moral attitudes and worldly conditions. But if I am not mistaken, there is no such thing as a will to beauty or a will to art. The essence of that particular will is its anonymity, its spontaneity, its complete lack of self-awareness.

But I am anticipating my conclusion. Let us return for a moment to the most fruitful field of research—to Gothic architecture. I have referred to some of the functional explanations of the form and structure of the Gothic cathedral and I might have mentioned many more. But when all possible explanations of this sort have been exhausted, the Gothic cathedral remains a unity outside the reach of our materialistic analysis. (Figs. 3, 6.) Its peculiarity resides in its suggestion of transcendental qualities—the sublimity of the idea of God, the infinite longing of mankind for goodness and beauty. These spiritual qualities are not embodied in specific symbols or concrete images: they emanate from the enfolded space, from the unending melody of line and surface, from a complex unity which was not the creation of one architect, nor even of one generation. They are slowly evolved, sometimes over a century or more, and what one man begins another will take over and develop, many men will develop in many directions, multiform in their activities but mysteriously uniform in their aim.

I have often protested against the popular misconception of the building of our ancient cathedrals. The great monuments of the Middle Ages were not the autonomous creation of a lot of rustic craftsmen. They had their qualified architects and clerks of works, and these were often very cultured and widely travelled men. A Gothic cathedral rarely has the unity we find in buildings of an earlier or a later period: it is an accretion of the work of many master-masons over two or three centuries. Where we can isolate and compare the work of an architect such as William of Sens or Bernard of Soissons, it bears the mark of his personality as much as any building of Palladio's or Sir Christopher Wren's. Admittedly the architects of the Middle Ages were in the grip of something bigger than themselves. But do not let us make that 'something' too big, too grandiose. It was in the first place a question of 'enthusiasm,' using the word in its eighteenth-century sense. The great cathedrals were often sponsored by building societies—bodies of a somewhat different character from the modern organizations which have usurped that name. Voluntary organizations were formed for the specific purpose of building a great church. Professor Coulton tells us that 'medieval chroniclers often notice briefly certain ways of enthusiasm which impelled whole populations, rich and poor, to labour together upon the town walls in times of danger, or upon some favoured church at a moment of livelier faith.'

Abbot Haimon's description of the building of the Norman

cathedrals of the twelfth century is well-known, but I may perhaps quote a sentence or two to give you the spirit of it. 'Whoever saw,' he wrote, 'whoever heard, in all the generations past, that kings, princes, mighty men of this world, puffed up with honours and riches, men and women of noble birth, should bind bridles upon their proud and swollen necks and submit them to waggons which, after the fashion of brute beasts, they dragged with their loads of wine, corn, oil, lime, stones, beams, and other things necessary to sustain life or build churches, even to Christ's abode? Moreover, as they draw the waggons we may see this miracle that, although sometimes a thousand men and women, or even more, are bound in the traces (so vast indeed in the mass, so great is the engine, and so heavy the load laid upon it), yet they go forward in such silence that no voice, no murmur, is heard; and, unless we saw it with our eyes, no man would dream that so great a multitude is there. When, again, they pause on the way, then no other voice is heard but confession of guilt, with supplication and pure prayer to God that He may vouchsafe pardon for their sins; and, while the priests there preach peace, hatred is soothed, discord is driven away, debts are forgiven, and unity is restored betwixt man and man.'[1]

Professor Coulton is famous for his caution, and he has debunked many sentimental legends about the Middle Ages; but he agrees with William Morris that the real strength of Gothic architecture arose from the fact that it was 'the people's art'. 'Everybody watched the people at work; everybody was interested in them . . .' and he adds, 'It is natural that, in our own time, artists and art lovers should look back regretfully at those simpler days, when there was not only greater unity of status among the workmen, but more unity of spirit between them and their public.'

[1] G. G. Coulton, *Life in the Middle Ages* (Cambridge, 1928–30), Vol. II, p. 19.

Art in general was a social activity, and though it was carried out by individual artists and craftsmen, it was not a private enterprise, a secret hobby. In such a period two apparently contradictory conditions coexist: a group consciousness which is coherent and therefore not too extensive—the city-state is the ideal unit; and an enterprise or rivalry among the constituent elements of this group. I know of no better description of the features of such a conjunction in its historical actuality than that given by Sismondi in his *History of the Italian Republics*, a work which has been unduly overshadowed by the later speculations of Burckhardt. At a point where he has reached the end of the thirteenth century, Sismondi pauses in his narrative to make some general observations on the characteristics of that vital epoch. I have translated a passage from the original French edition;[1] it is not so well-known as it deserves to be and I will quote it at some length:

'During the struggle of the citizens, first with the nobles and then with the people, civil liberty was no doubt frequently violated; the rights which men reserved to themselves by the social contract, and whose guarantee has even been the sole aim of their association, were more than once disregarded: nevertheless, in the midst of this disorder, while civil liberty succumbed, democratic liberty still remained. This latter consists, not of guarantees, but of powers; it does not assure to nations peace, or order, or economy, or prudence; but is its own reward. It is, for the citizen who has once known it, the sweetest of enjoyments, thus to influence the destiny of his country, to have a share in sovereignty, above all to put himself immediately under the law and to recognize no authorities but those he has himself created. This manner of coming out of oneself to live in common, to feel in common, to become part of a great whole, uplifts a man and makes him capable of great things. Political passions make more heroes than individual

[1] Actually the revised edition of 1826, Chap. XXV, pp. 169–72.

passions; and though the connection may not be immediately apparent, they also make more artists, more poets, more philosophers, more scientists. The century whose history we have just finished supplies the proof. In the midst of the convulsions of its civil wars, Florence renewed its architecture, sculpture and painting; it produced the greatest poet which even unto this day Italy can boast; it restored philosophy to a position of honour; it gave an encouragement to the sciences which was copied by all the free cities of Italy, and established in the place of barbarism an epoch of fine art and culture.'

Sismondi then turns to the particular subject we are considering:

'The first of the fine arts which was reborn in Italy in the Middle Ages was architecture. Since imitation is not its aim, and architecture rises above created objects to represent the ideal forms of symmetrical and abstract beauty such as man conceives them, it is of all the fine arts the one which best enables us to know the grandeur, the energy or the insignificance of the nation where it has flourished, of the man who has carried it out. It is the art that most easily transmits the heritage of preceding generations and that for which genius and will-power best make up for the little secrets, little techniques and little rules which must be observed in all the other arts and which one must study before beginning to create. . . . The imposing cathedral of Florence, and a hundred more equally sumptuous edifices, which were founded in the thirteenth century by the Italian republics, preserve the memory of these free and generous peoples, to whom history, so far, has rendered scant justice.

'The architecture of the thirteenth century bears in quite another sense the imprint of the customs of the time: it is completely republican, destined essentially for communal use and communal enjoyment. City walls, palaces of the commune, churches open to everyone, canals which spread fertility to a whole district, all have been built in this century. The multiplicity of such works, undertaken at the same time in all cities of Italy, shows that emulation between similar governments is much more favourable to the fine arts than the luxury of monarchs; that the spirit of the communities, where even private homes are built under the eyes of the people, gives more encouragement to architects than the spirit of monarchies, where even public edifices are built under the eyes of the prince; for in the end artists are more flattered to receive the applause and admiration of their fellow citizens than the approval and payment of a master.' (Figs. 7*a*, 7*b*, 8*a*.)

Though this explanation of the greatness of great architecture can be reconciled with Strzygowski's emphasis on the local origins of art, it is entirely inconsistent with the racial theory put forward by many historians of culture and by totalitarian politicians like Hitler, who would correlate the greatness of architecture with national greatness, with racial expansion. For such a theory we find no evidence in the past, where, as we have seen, the correlation is rather with the small city-state. Nor, indeed, do we find any positive evidence for such a theory in the present. I hesitate to bring the typical architecture of America into question, but I have the authority of its leading practitioners for casting doubt on its aesthetic value. We know Frank Lloyd Wright's view, and may dismiss it as eccentric. But how disenchanted are the arch-creators of this style. Here, for example, is the voice of Dr. Harvey Corbett: 'I recall many years ago being asked to serve on a competition jury for a proposed church in New Jersey. The other members of the jury were also New York architects. We took a ferry-boat from West Twenty-third Street and went down the Hudson to make our train connection, and as we sat out on the upper deck we looked east, observing the then sky-line of New York which was well on its way to its present silhouette but still some distance from reaching that multiplicity of pinnacles which it has now attained.

(Fig. 10*c*.) I asked my architectural confreres if ten of the greatest brains of the nation were to go to work conscientiously to create the most involved, complicated, and disorderly mess which their combined genius could produce—did they believe by any stretch of the imagination such a group of brains could ever approximate the mess we were looking at? We all agreed it couldn't be done.'[1]

As for the British Empire, on which the sun never sets, quantitatively the greatest imperial power the world has ever known—its characteristic architecture is the industrial slum. Only in small states like Switzerland, Finland and Holland (Figs. 8*b*, 9*b*) do we see the tentative approach towards an original architectural style: a movement to which the people themselves contribute understanding and encouragement. Significantly, the modern architecture of these small states is again, as was Greek architecture and Gothic architecture, an international and not a national style. Nothing could have less justification than that opposition to modern architecture, typical of nationalistic states like Germany and Russia, which bases itself on its international character. All great architectural styles have been international: that is only another way of expressing the obvious fact that all great architecture is universal in its appeal. But the roots are in the local soil. We should realize the fundamental paradox of the process which brings about this result. Intensive co-operation breaks through to collective consciousness: local pressures yield universal values.

The greatness of great architecture is not to be explained by

[1] Harvey Corbett, 'The Skyscraper and the Automobile Have Made the Modern City', in *Studies in the Arts and Architecture* (University of Pennsylvania Press, 1941). Dr. Corbett also confesses (p. 109): 'Personally I am not so keen about skyscrapers as I used to be, I am just finishing out two of them in New York at the present moment; perhaps these will be among the last of those multi-storied monstrosities of which we Americans seem to be so proud.'

national greatness: its secret is not to be found in race, not in blood, not in soil, not even in religion, but in a certain social structure animated by a spirit which may be religious or may be political, but which essentially owes its efficacy to its integrity—its wholeness and smallness, its all-over-ness and intimacy. The generation of enthusiasm is the necessary postulate; but the means come from relatively simple factors, which, because they are so simple, have generally been overlooked—from mutual aid, from the social cohesiveness of small groups, from unity of sentiment and unity of aim.

Here it may be objected that one of our two great epochs of architecture—the Greek—was the characteristic expression of a society by no means integrated in this sense. It was a society based on the institution of slavery. Far be it from me to defend such an anomaly, but at least do not let us be frightened unduly by a word which has acquired all sorts of implications which it never had for the Greeks. The complacency of otherwise humane philosophers like Plato and Aristotle towards this barbarous social custom has always been a puzzle to the modern age, but we must realize that the Greek slave, however disenfranchised from the benefits of citizenship in the city-state, was never an ostracized creature such as, for example, the American or African Negro is to-day. The class constituted one half or more of the inhabitants of the city-state, and their human rights and personal liberties were fully guaranteed by law. I doubt whether a Greek slave would have exchanged his position for that of a worker in a modern munitions factory. He would have been outraged by a social phenomenon like our mass unemployment. I am not a classical scholar, but as far as I can gather from our general knowledge of the subject, the Greek slave was very definitely integrated into the society of which he formed such an essential part. His status was inferior, in the political sense, but it was definite. He was a recognized unit in the social structure and, whether a labourer or an artisan, could take part in, and take pride in, the city's achievements.[1] He could rise to greatness, like Epictetus, and still remain a slave. I cannot see that he differed much from his fellow-labourers and artisans in the Middle Ages, who equally had no political status, no political power, but did enjoy what the modern worker can hardly be said to possess: responsible status in the economic structure of the community.

Many factors must doubtless come to the same crux: size and exclusiveness of the community, civic consciousness, religious unity, group integrity, guild organization and the artist's personal responsibility for his work. The unlikelihood of securing the co-operation or conjunction of so many complex factors at one and the same time is a sufficient explanation of the rarity of great epochs in architecture. Nor can we assume that such a conjunction will automatically call into being artists adequate for the occasion. We like to think that the great occasion always finds its fit exponent; and there may be biological and historical evidence for such a belief. But finally it is a question of faith in creative evolution. We may feel that history is a meaningless process, inane, repetitive and essentially arbitrary. The artist who achieves his personal integration in a great work of art is then but an evolutionary sport, a chance thrown up on the wastes of time. But if we feel that an obscure purpose or design can be read into 'the goings-on of the universe', as Wordsworth rather disparagingly called them, then the appearance of great art is not an arbitrary phenomenon: it is the highest point of the evolutionary process, the emergent apex of human development, and as such is explained by laws as rational as those which explain any other biological growth. We cannot ex-

[1] Cf. Gustave Glotz, *Ancient Greece at Work* (London, 1926) for a detailed account of the organization of industry and labour in Athens and other Greek cities.

pect in our present state of knowledge to tabulate those laws; but at least we can discern some of the environmental factors which favour their operation; and freedom with fraternity is the real substance of them.

Whatever the positive connection between the form of social organization and the quality of architecture, it is certain that in the negative direction the loss of social unity always involves a stylistic decadence. The quality of Greek architecture begins to decline from the moment labour becomes a commodity, and the artist a man of business. The quality of medieval architecture began to decline from the moment that same sense of social unity was lost. 'As time went on,' writes Professor Coulton, 'something like modern capitalism was developed.'[1] The contractor appeared on the scene, with his stereotyped designs and his gangs of uninspired craftsmen. Personal expression, individual responsibility, the autonomy of voluntary associations, the articulation of the political structure from the simple to the composite—these disappeared as the power of capital became concentrated in the strongly centralized state and the cities lost their autonomy.

Well, that is another long story which has often been told and which I will not repeat. But without adopting a political attitude we may conclude, quite dispassionately, that great art, in particular great architecture, depends on the presence of those sociological factors which I have described and which we do in fact find most evident where architecture is most evidently great—in the Hellenic civilization of the sixth and fifth centuries B.C. and in the Middle Ages in Europe. The individual artist is as necessary to the birth of a work of art as the individual woman is to the birth of a child. Each process has its laws of conception, gestation and parturition. But just as laws of genetics and heredity, of dietetics and climate, influence the personality of the individual child, so various

[1] *Medieval Panorama* (Cambridge, 1938), pp. 569–70.

social factors influence the character of a work of art. What I have tried to do in this lecture is to determine the social factors most favourable to the creative functions of the artist in the particular art of architecture. The practical conclusion I have reached is the same as that reached by Walter Gropius by an entirely different method of analysis: 'The key for a successful rebuilding of our post-war communities is our determination to let the human element become the dominant factor.'[1]

Admittedly I have presented you with a problem rather than with that problem's solution. I think the sociologists should be able to isolate the social factors involved, and necessarily involved, in great architecture. But the actual process by means of which these qualities are translated into a language of form—their plastic equivalents or spatial equivalents—that process belongs to the psychology of the individual. The most we can venture to assert is that when the individual will is in unison with the general will, when the personal consciousness merges into group consciousness, then a transformation takes place. The group is more powerful than the individual, not only in the physical sense, but in spiritual potentiality. It has this power only in virtue of achieving group-consciousness, which is not the same thing as consciousness-of-being-a-group. When a psychological unity of consciousness is achieved by a group, then that group has reached the highest evolutionary level, and its artists are inspired to works of art which are an expression of its vital achievement.

I do not wish to end on a note of scientific agnosticism. I merely suggest that the sociologist must at this point hand over the problem to the psychologist. But though we may reach understanding of the problem by methods of psychological analysis, we shall not recreate the conditions of great architecture, if that is our aim, except by methods of synthesis. We must create a social structure that

[1] *Rebuilding Our Communities* (Chicago, 1945), p. 16.

will ensure the interplay of individual freedom and mutual aid. As for the enthusiasm which is also necessary, that spontaneous grace descended in equal potency on a small Greek colony at Paestum and on a small rural community at Chartres, on an oriental outpost in Europe (Fig. 10*b*) like Edirne (Adrianople) and on a German fortress-city like Ulm (Fig. 10*a*). The religious spirit and political ideals of these two groups had nothing in common. Religiously speaking they were antithetical; politically speaking, their ideologies were, to say the least of it, dissimilar. What they had in common was a sociological structure—in fact, using the word in its strict sociological sense, their communism: and it is from an analysis of the nature of this sociological factor that we must learn the secret of great architecture, of all great art.

IV

The Irrelevance of Realism

A controversy, which promises to be as prolonged and bitter as that which rent the Christian church many centuries ago, has been smouldering in our midst for about forty years. It has little or nothing to do with religion, and we have not been using the same terminology as the theologians of the eighth century. Nevertheless it is perhaps fundamentally the same controversy, and underneath their garb of psychology or politics, the modern attitudes do not differ greatly from those of the ancient protagonists.

In the Iconoclastic Controversy one party objected to realistic images because it was felt that the associations they established in the mind of the beholder were too sensuous, and precluded a spiritual relationship with God. The other party held that the senses were gateways to the realm of the spirit, and that the contemplation of images induced in the beholder feelings of reverence and adoration. There was also a suggestion of a class distinction—we clerks, we learned people, may be capable of direct communion with the Holy Spirit, but for the illiterate and unlearned multitude visual aids may be necessary.

God is absent from the present controversy. The only philosophy involved is a materialistic one, but as we shall see, Tolstoy provides a link between the old controversy and the new one. There is also this difference—the ancient controversy was for or against all imagery, whereas the modern controversy opposes two types of imagery—realistic and formal, figurative and non-figurative. But actually the old iconoclasts allowed the use of abstract symbols and of non-figurative ornament, so perhaps the difference is not so great after all.

Nowadays it is only when art is widely advertised and, one may suspect, when its monetary value is declared in sufficiently startling terms, that the public awakens from its usual aesthetic apathy and expresses its feelings. These are usually feelings of outrage. Its reactions to the results of the International Sculpture Competition of 1953 were in this respect typical. An anonymous donor had offered a number of prizes, the highest of which, though not equal to the annual salary of a judge or an average company director, seemed enormous when destined for an artist. A jury of experts (museum directors, art critics, professors of art history) had awarded this prize to a work of art (Figs. 15, 16) which completely failed to 'register', as a work of art, with the journalists and with the public they represent. A controversy ensued in which the distance separating the artist from the public was once more revealed as infinite and apparently unbridgeable.

If it had served no other purpose, the Competition would have been worth while because it brought this conflict to the surface in extremely poignant terms. It was a competition open to all comers, but limited to one form of plastic expression (sculpture) and to the representation of a definite theme of universal significance. An art of our time had been challenged in an unescapable manner. The theme was worthy of the deepest commitment, and no form of treatment was excluded. In the event, almost every conceivable manner of treatment was attempted—every style, traditional or experimental, was to be found among the entries. It is not possible to say that the jury might have reached a different judgment if some other style had been represented: all styles were represented, but the only adequate style, in the opinion of the jury, was one which the public has found too extreme, too incomprehensible—a specifically modern style.

Let me note here, however, that though the twelve prize-winners might all be described, in journalistic phraseology, as 'modernistic', they did in fact represent several distinct styles within the contemporary language of plastic expression. Elements of such mutually exclusive styles as constructivism, naturalism and surrealism were dominant in one or another of the selected models: but for the public such refinements do not exist, or do not matter—all the models were equally 'modernistic' and equally incomprehensible.

I am using a term, the 'public', which I use with reluctance, and without any snobbish implication. What we mean by the term is public opinion as expressed by and in the press: the opinions of journalists and of individuals who take the trouble to write to the press—an infinitesimal proportion of the whole people, who on such occasions always remain either indifferent or dumb. One may legitimately despise the press without despising the public it caters for; and one may despise the critics who express their personal views in the press but we need not necessarily identify their ignorance or lack of vision with the general policy of the journals they work for. Where art is concerned, there is a complete lack of coherence and integrity in the press. A journal that is conservative in politics may be represented by a progressive art critic; a progressive journal may be represented by a conservative art critic. Journalistically, art is not a question of serious policy; art is 'classified' as one of the 'entertainments', and the art critic is usually a jester. Like many jesters, he often conceals beneath his motley the bitterness of a disappointed and vindictive nature.

We have, therefore, a vocal public which is represented by a few critics and publicists of very doubtful integrity; and a mute and much larger public which does not express itself and may be indifferent. I am not going to pretend that the mute public could be induced to express an opinion on art contrary to the opinion of the press, though in politics it does so in no uncertain terms. The divorce of the arts from the people is an obvious feature of our civilization—it is recognized in such terms as 'highbrow' and 'lowbrow', and in the provision in British broadcasting of three programmes for three levels of culture. Between the extremes of these levels there is no communication and no possibility of communication. The same distinct strata exist in literature, in the theatre, the cinema, and even in the press: the gulf between *The Times* and the *Daily Express* is also not bridgeable.

In most of the arts it is a case of 'live and let live', but for some obscure reason there is no complacent tolerance for the highbrow painter or sculptor. The public—the vocal public—always assumes that when an artist exhibits a picture, he has thrown a pot of paint at them. A piece of sculpture is a graven image which excites all their iconoclastic impulses. I suspect that such impulses come from some deep level of the unconscious. Art itself, directly or indirectly, comes from that same source, and the unconscious does not like to see its secrets betrayed. Art is an indecent exposure of the unconscious—so down with art! I would commend this subject to our psychologists; we need an analysis of the iconoclastic complex.

This is a tragic situation inseparable from our cultural heritage and it is not for the artist to resolve it by direct means. Art is not an instrument of propaganda or persuasion: in that respect it is as ineffective as science or reason. An integrated culture, such as produces an integrated art, and a people integrated with its artists, evolves organically out of the appropriate conditions: it is not produced by the conscious will of any minority, such as the clerics, the intellectuals, the artists of a period: it is not produced by the conscious will of a society as a whole. It is only when it exists, or after it has existed, that we can discern the conditions which gave rise to an integrated culture. We can try, as statesmen, economists, sociologists and philosophers, to identify and analyse the processes which have led to our present condition of disintegration: we have our own ideas about the conditions necessary for a new world, a new civilization. But these ideas are contradictory, and cannot all be true. History will take its course: a vital cyclic process beyond human control. As artists we can define, illuminate and even mitigate this process, but in the wider prospect we must wait for the blind resolutions of economic necessity, permitting ourselves a faint hope that one day these will restore the conditions for an integrated culture. Meanwhile the duty of the artist is to preserve art from the contamination of the false values, political values and propagandist values, utilitarian values and entertainment values—all the false values that destroy the integrity and the universality of the work of art.

The artist who maintains the values of art is accused of living in an ivory tower. It is true that he does live in isolation, and that he has been compelled to build defences which may have a tower-like appearance. Art is everywhere on the defensive because it is everywhere attacked by the false values I have mentioned, and its most dangerous enemies are those who have penetrated its defences—critics who have persuaded the artist to conform to some political ideology, to commit himself to an ideology of art inspired by political motives.

This demand for the commitment, or 'engagement', of the artist, though it originated in communist ideology, and more specifically in the events which followed the Revolution in Russia, has now been given a wider interpretation. The same demand was made on artists by the Nazis in Germany and the Fascists in Italy, and even by the Resistance Movement in France and elsewhere. Wherever political passions become violent and take to arms, there an attempt is made to enlist the artist in the struggle—art becomes, not only an instrument of propaganda, but also a social function which must be completely indentified with the political ideology in question.

We are at once struck by the fact that whatever the political ideology may be—socialist, fascist, communist, or MacCarthyist—and however inconsistent these political doctrines may be one with another, all express one opinion about art. It must be realist. All condemn the more specifically modern forms of art as formalist, as obscure, as degenerate, as escapist, and so on.

We should first ask, what do such people mean by 'realism'. Like most of the terms used in the history of culture, it is an extremely ambiguous word. In philosophy it is opposed to nominalism or conceptualism and denotes the doctrine that universals 'or general ideas' have objective existence; or it is opposed to idealism as the belief that matter as the object of perception has real existence. From this latter philosophical meaning it slides off into popular use to indicate 'things as they really are', and may thus be a vigorous use of language, a refusal to mince matters, as we say, and so comes to indicate actions which conform to such a spirit. During the nineteenth century the term acquired a further nuance, more particularly in association with literature and painting. In painting it indicated a precise rendering of details, and a refusal to reject subjects because they do not conform to some ideal; in this sense the term 'naturalism' was sometimes substituted. In literature the meaning was very much the same, but with an implication that the details of reality are usually mean and sordid.

Realism in philosophy is still a living force—its last great representative was Whitehead. But realism in this sense has nothing whatsoever to do with the conflict we are discussing. The epistemological use of the word, however, has some relevance—the belief that sense-experience 'reports a true and uninterrupted, if limited, account of objects; that it is possible to have faithful and direct knowledge of the actual world' (Runes: *Dictionary of Philosophy*). There are artists to-day who believe that it is their function to give a true account of the actual world, an account that is superior to colour-photography because, presumably, a mechanical instrument is not yet as perfect as the human sensibility—not so exact as a recording instrument. But again, this is not the meaning involved in the present controversy, though it is not irrelevant.

The realist in the discussion of contemporary art is combining two distinct claims, neither of which is realistic in any of the accepted meanings of the word. In the first place he is demanding that art should be easily readable: that its significance, its account of the actual world, should be unambiguous, clear, and acceptable to everyman as evidence. The man in the street should be in a position to say: No, this is not good art because it does not correspond with the evidence of my senses. If other people agree with him, then the work of art will be condemned. Presumably if not all the people in the street agree with him, it would be a question of a majority vote, or of an official pronouncement—such pronouncements are actually made in Russia.

But into this fairly simple and very naive conception of realism, the self-styled realists import another meaning—a meaning which is selective. In effect, they define what they mean by 'the actual world' and it is an arbitrary definition. Only that part of the world is actual, they say, which consists of 'local, urgently everyday issues'. This particular definition we owe to Mr. John Berger,[1] and I do not wish to attach too much importance to what is a personal point of view. But it is nevertheless a point of view which is official in Russia, and which is the unexpressed view of many

[1] In an article or letter contributed to *The New Statesman and Nation*.

people elsewhere in the world—people who would not call themselves communists or have intention of aligning themselves on any ideological front. Art, such people might say, is not for an élite—not for a minority of any kind: it must therefore not only be understandable to everyman—it must also solicit and arouse everyman's interest. In order to do this it must deal with these local and urgent everyday issues—everyday issues for everyman's taste. Such exponents of realism in art specifically reject all forms of universalism in art, perhaps because they are aware, more or less consciously, that universalism inevitably leads to forms of art which are not readily accessible to the man in the street.

It is a curious fact that in all the recent discussions of this subject the name of Tolstoy has never been mentioned. Yet Tolstoy, in his last great polemical work, *What is Art*? went to the heart of the matter with a care and a profundity that have never been surpassed. I have, on previous occasions, criticized Tolstoy's argument. I still think that it is based on a false premiss—on a false definition of the creative process in art. Tolstoy regarded art as a means of transmission, or communication; and what it transmits, or communicates, he said, is a genuine emotion experienced by the artist. He conveys this identical emotion into the hearts or understanding of others, so that they too experience it. Technical competence is taken for granted, and the value of the work of art is simply the value of transmitted experience. This logically implies a moral valuation of art, and from this Tolstoy did not shrink: in the end art must be judged by the moral standards of a Christian community.

This theory of art is mistaken in my view because of the underlying assumption that the true work of art is always understood, always understandable. When Tolstoy defines art as the transmission of feeling, he always has in mind specific human emotions—good emotions or bad emotions, emotions of love or of pride, feelings of truth or of falsity, and he always thinks of these emotions or feelings as social, as everyday experiences. But the artist, says Tolstoy, has to make a choice—he has to choose the good feelings in his breast and reject the bad ones, and in order to make this choice he must be good Christian, for Christianity represents the highest stage in the development of a moral consciousness by mankind. Tolstoy has often been represented as a puritanical contemner of art: on the contrary, Tolstoy gives art the highest function in human society. 'Art', he says, 'is not a pleasure, a solace, or an amusement; art is a great matter. Art is an organ of human life transmitting man's reasonable perception into feeling. In our age the common religious perception of men is the consciousness of the brotherhood of man—we know that the well-being of man lies in union with his fellowmen. True science should indicate the various methods of applying this consciousness to life. Art should transform this perception into feeling.

'The task of art is enormous. Through the influence of real art, aided by science, guided by religion, that peaceful co-operation of man which is now maintained by external means—by our law-courts, police, charitable institutions, factory inspection, and so forth—should be obtained by man's free and joyous activity. Art should cause violence to be set aside.'

'And it is only art that can accomplish this.'[1]

I wish I could believe it—with all my heart I wish I could believe that art is capable of establishing the brotherhood of man. But I cannot believe it because I cannot believe that art performs its miracles in that way—I cannot believe that art functions by transforming states of mind (the reasonable perceptions of religion or science) into states of feeling. Art works the other way round. It begins with states of feeling, usually obscure states of feeling, and

[1] *What is Art?* trans. by Aylmer Maude (World's Classics edition, 1930), pp. 286–7.

it gives them concrete reality—it materializes them. It does this in various guises, but not necessarily in a form that can be immediately understood by the reasoning mind. Art usually transforms a specific feeling into a specific symbol—the feeling finds its equivalence in a plastic image. This image may be easily comprehensible, as when maternal love is represented by a mother with a child at her breast. But this is not necessarily the only way of representing the feeling of maternal love, and maternal love is not the only kind of love. Love in general is an extremely various and complex feeling, and has given rise to the greatest variety of works of art—from the lyrics of Sappho or the Symposium of Plato to the songs of Burns or Proust's great novel. Tolstoy would say that some of the feelings of love transmitted by some of these works of art are immoral feelings, and that therefore the work of art that transmits them is bad—the product of a decadent civilization. But how can one say that Sappho is a bad poet or Proust a bad novelist? Only by exercising a moral judgment—a judgment that has nothing to do with the substance or the validity of art. Only by imposing a moral duty on the artist, a duty which has no bearing on his technical duty, which is to create a work of art.

'All works of art', says the advocate of realist art, 'are bound directly or indirectly to be weapons.' This is true in the sense that any pebble, whatever its shape, will create a ripple when thrown into a pond. But the realist seems to argue that a stone of the right shape will create the kind of ripple we want. This is contrary to the nature of things—the shape of the work of art cannot be controlled by an external force, and remain a genuine work of art; nor does a ripple on the surface of the pond transform the pond's inner nature. Art is an individual activity—by no means can we get away from that basic fact—even a communal dance must have its choreographer if it has to attain any aesthetic form, and not be a mere rout. Assuming for a moment that it is the function of art to transmit feeling, then it must be recognized that the individual artist can transmit only such feelings as stir in his own breast. These feelings may be of a kind which can be shared with other people—feelings of patriotism or of brotherly love; but even in that case the artist does not transmit a general emotion, but his own feelings about a general situation—one man's patriotism, we might say, is another man's poison, and some people's conceptions of brotherly love are merely embarrassing. One man's conception of political imprisonment, as an incident at the Tate Gallery proved, can be another man's conception of an emotional insult.

The virtue of a symbol lies, and always did lie, in a relative degree of unintelligibility. A symbol loses its grip once its significance has been rationalized, and it has become generally understood. But so long as it remains unintelligible, it can, if it is a good symbol, exercise astonishing powers. These powers are by no means necessarily confined to a restricted circle of initiates—the effectiveness of symbols is in fact proportionate to their collectivity—to the range of significance they have for the collective unconscious. The more we consider the comparative history of civilizations, the more apparent it becomes that art is a complex symbolic activity, conforming to certain archetypal patterns and repeating with variations the same mythical themes. The whole course of art bears no correspondence to the guided, intentional, conscious activity envisaged by Tolstoy and the realists of our own time: it is a movement as vast as the tides of the ocean, uncontrollable by any conscious agencies, sucking social forms and conventions into its ebb and flow, but never creative of those forms and conventions. Art cannot create anything but its own symbolic forms, and these forms are not symbolic of any external ideas, but of the artist's own intuitions, feelings and fantasies.

What goes on in the artist's mind cannot be accounted for by the simple psychology of perception and expression on which

Tolstoy relied. What kind of psychology a latter-day realist like Mr. Berger relies on is not clear—something equally naive, I would suppose, but not so simple. I do not wish to transfer the argument to a psychological plane, but it must be made quite clear that the realist theory of art does rely on a very naive psychological basis. Tolstoy was not ignorant of the psychology of his time—he quotes Spencer, Grant Allen, Véron and Sully, who in 1896 represented the best scientific standards of psychology. But since that time a Copernican revolution has taken place in psychology—in anthropology, too—and it simply will not do to rely on the notion that the mind is formed and directed by sense impressions only. Tolstoy quotes what he calls Véron's 'experimental definition of art'—the theory that 'art is the external manifestation, by means of lines, colours, movements, sounds, or words, of emotions felt by man', and rejects it, not as we might do, on the grounds that 'emotions' is an inadequte term to describe the mental states which art does represent, but on the grounds that such 'external manifestations by means of lines, colours, etc.' *may not act on others*. If there is a failure of transmission, then there is no art. Tolstoy does not allow for a successful transmission of emotions by such means—he merely assumes that such means—lines, colours, movements, sounds or words—are not in themselves adequate as 'the means of intercourse between man and man'. The means of intercourse must be a language understandable on the rational level of discourse. If visual art is in question, then the images must be, not symbols expressing what is verbally inexpressible, but pictorial illustrations of moving experiences. The value of the work of art will then clearly emerge from the nature of the experience depicted. Tolstoy gives two examples from the English Academy of 1897 which makes his meaning very clear, and which I will therefore quote:

'In the English Academy of 1897 two pictures were exhibited together; one of these, by J. C. Dollman, was the temptation of St.

Anthony (Fig. 13). The Saint is on his knees praying. Behind him stands a naked woman and animals of some kind. It is apparent that the naked woman pleased the artist very much, but that Anthony did not concern him at all, and that so far from the temptation being terrible to him (the artist) it is highly agreeable. Therefore if there be any art in this picture, it is very nasty and false. Next in the same book of academy pictures comes a picture by Langley (Fig. 14), showing a stray beggar boy, who has evidently been called in by a woman who has taken pity on him. The boy, pitifully drawing his bare feet under the bench, is eating; the woman is looking on, probably considering whether he will not want some more; and a girl of about seven, leaning on her arm, is carefully and seriously looking on, not taking her eyes from the hungry boy and evidently understanding for the first time what poverty is and what inequality among people is, and asking herself why she has everything provided for her while this boy goes barefoot and hungry? She feels sorry and yet pleased, and she loves both the boy and goodness. . . . One feels that the artist loved this girl and that she too loves. And this picture, by an artist who, I think, is not very widely known, is an admirable and true work of art.'[1]

I quote this passage from Tolstoy's *What is Art*? at length, not to make fun of it, but to reveal in all its naivety the sentimental basis for the so-called realist theory of art. If it is 'reality' in any acceptable meaning of the word, that art should represent, then there is as much reality in a naked woman, and in Mr. Dollman's feelings of admiration for her beauty, as there is in a hungry beggar boy and Mr. Langley's love for the little girl who pities him. In Tolstoy's comparison of these two pictures, an aesthetic criterion does not arise and therefore is not applied. We have only a distinction of the feelings experienced and illustrated by two individuals

[1] *What is Art?* trans. by Aylmer Maude (World's Classics edition, 1930), pp. 224–5.

equally skilful in depicting scenes which illustrate emotional situations. According to the criterion applied by Tolstoy, which is an ethical criterion, it is wicked to admire a naked woman and good to feel pity for a hungry beggar boy. And with this criterion he proceeded to condemn most of the works of art commonly regarded as masterpieces by people with any aesthetic sensibility.

Moral sensibility and aesthetic sensibility—those are the basic terms of our conflict. The communist realist of to-day has shifted his ground; his sentimentality is political rather than ethical. But when he criticizes a work of art he uses exactly the same methods as Tolstoy: he ignores the aesthetic criterion and applies a criterion that is essentially moral. We are no longer moved by hungry beggar boys, but we are moved by the victims of fascism, or even by the victims of communism. Poverty is no longer an urgent theme, but tyranny is. So the artist should depict scenes which show the tyrant as ugly, his victim as pitiable; he should hate the one and love the other, and his feelings should be shown in scenes that are immediately apprehensible by the simplest intelligence. The revolutionary struggle of the twentieth century is rich in such themes; the artist must identify himself with the morally good side in this struggle and use his skill to ensure the triumph of the good.

It is a simple faith, and to anyone who sympathizes, as I do, with Tolstoy's social ethics, it would be easy to feel tolerant towards it but for one sure fact—it means the death of art. Art is not and never has been subordinate to moral values. Moral values are social values; aesthetic values are human values. Moral values promote and protect a particular way of life; aesthetic values promote and protect life itself, as a vital principle. Moral values are based on sentiments, that is to say, on clear notions of goodness or happiness; aesthetic values are based on intuitions and feelings, that is to say, on obscure reactions to experience. Morality seeks to restrain the feelings, art seeks to define them by externalizing them, by giving them significant form. Morality has only one aim—the ideal good; art has quite another aim—the objective truth. Morality finds expression in precept and commandment; art in symbol and myth. The moralist preaches or prophesies; the artist bears witness, impassively. Morals change with time and economy—chastity and pity were not always virtues; art never changes—the drawings of palaeolithic man, the tragedies of Greece, the cathedrals of the Middle Ages, the love songs of the Renaissance—these are timeless and eternally human and wonderful.

There are people who will admit this fundamental distinction, people who will reject one aspect of Tolstoy's doctrine (that art must have a moral purpose) and who will nevertheless cling to the other aspect of this doctrine (that art must be so clear and simple in its expression that its appeal is universal). True art, Tolstoy held, should be accessible to all men; only on that condition could art fulfil its great unifying function.

Again one must sympathize with the motive. Tolstoy felt that the art of our own time had become a separate and sophisticated art, the art of the upper, educated classes; and that this isolation of art from the daily life of the masses had resulted in an ingrowing of techniques, a development of refinements and complexities of no great significance in themselves, but effectively divorcing art from the people at large.

In the grip of this belief, Tolstoy did not hesitate to condemn the whole evolution of music from the time of the invention of harmony and counterpoint (he roundly declared that Beethoven's *Ninth Symphony* is a bad work of art); he condemned the arts of painting and sculpture as we know them, excepting only certain genre-subjects, animal paintings and china dolls; and he likewise condemned all modern literature, including his own works except for two stories (*God sees the Truth but Waits* and *A Prisoner of the Caucasus*). The modern realist would not go quite so far; but

Tolstoy was honest and logical. Once you accept the view that art must be accessible to all men, art must be reduced to the level of china dolls. It must become peasant art: 'the epic of Genesis, the Gospel parables, folk-legends, fairy-tales, and folk songs . . .'; or when Tolstoy becomes more specific, 'the *Iliad*, the *Odyssey*, the stories of Isaac, Jacob, and Joseph . . . the story of Sakya Muni and the hymns of the Vedas . . .'

There is a certain disingenuousness in the argument at this point. The masses for whom Tolstoy is so solicitous do not read the *Iliad* and the *Odyssey* (in spite of Pelican editions), and scarcely anyone in the Western World reads the story of Sakya Muni and the hymns of the Vedas. These works survive as classics from remote civilizations and though they are not lacking in narrative interest, and in human interest, it needs historical imagination and a certain power of concentration—a contracting out of urgent, everyday issues—to read such works with any real enjoyment. The taste for folk-legends and folk-songs is now a very sophisticated one—folk art in general has to be kept alive by artificial aid. Folk art disappeared with the 'folk': there is no art of the masses—never has been and never will be. There are various more or less unconscious accretions of fable and legend—often derived from a higher level of culture—but these belong largely to the epochs before the invention of printing, and had depended for their survival on verbal transmission—they owe their simplicity and vividness to that necessity. The *Iliad* and the *Odyssey* are major examples of this kind of art, as the Border Ballads are a late and minor example. To make modern art conform to this pre-literary standard of transmission would be to ignore all these developments of technique and knowledge which have made the modern world possible. There would be arguments just as logical for returning to the morals and the social economy of the ancient Greeks or Jews.

Tolstoy weakens his argument when he appeals to history. Its real strength lies in the claim that great art proceeds from the fundamental characteristics of human nature, and that these characteristics do not change. This claim we must admit, but we must then go on to assert, against Tolstoy and against the modern realists and populists, that human nature is a very complex entity—the most complex entity in the whole creation. To reveal and appraise the fundamental characteristics of an entity so complex has demanded, and still demands, instruments of increasing refinement and exactitude. Homer may reveal a fundamental trait in one of his heroes by means of a vivid phrase or image—and that gives us great pleasure. Shakespeare, in order to reveal the character of Hamlet (in a play which Tolstoy considered a false imitation of a work of art) requires many more and much more subtle images, and our pleasure is all the intenser. Dostoevsky, Tolstoy himself in works which he renounced, Henry James, Proust—all these writers use an increasing degree of complexity and range of reference to explore what are still fundamental characteristics of human nature. We can say the same of our great painters and musicians—of Van Gogh and Cézanne, of Schönberg and Stravinsky—they are all using their sensibilities, sensibilities of great refinement and exactitude, to depict fundamental characteristics of human nature. But the people, the masses, do not look; they do not listen; they do not understand. Is it the art, then, that is wrong, as Tolstoy and the contemporary realists say; or is it the people?

It is, more accurately speaking, neither the art nor the people; it is the civilization itself that is wrong. It is not merely that a class structure of society produces different types of people with different interests—a similar class structure existed in ancient Greece and India, in all the civilizations that produced the few works of art admired by Tolstoy. We must face the fact that any society will exhibit wide variations of human intelligence and sensibility. Tolstoy himself once said: 'Society resembles a crystal. No matter

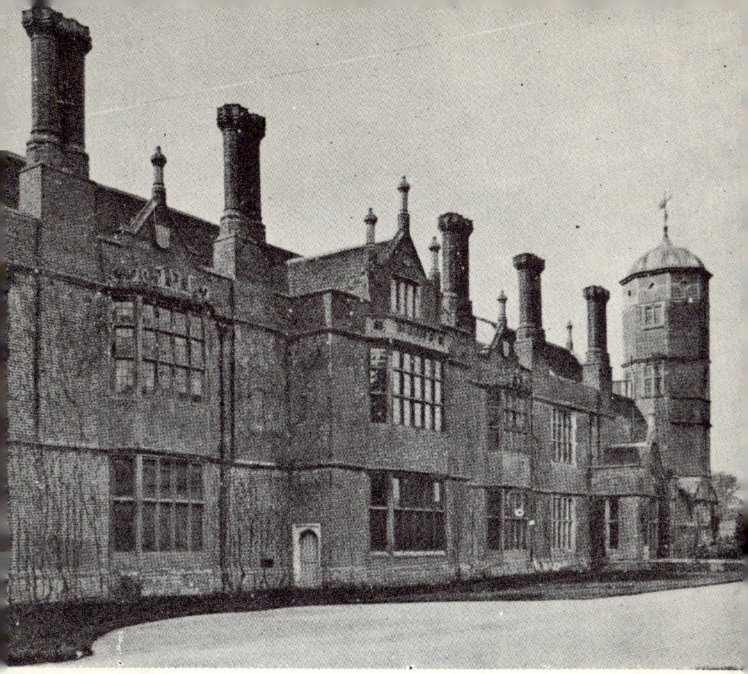

1. Cobham Hall, Kent. About 1595

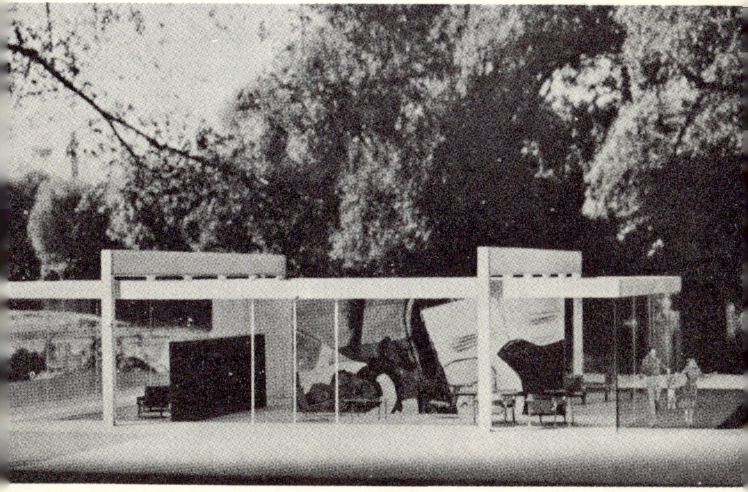

2. Project for a house. Architect: Mies van der Rohe. 1952

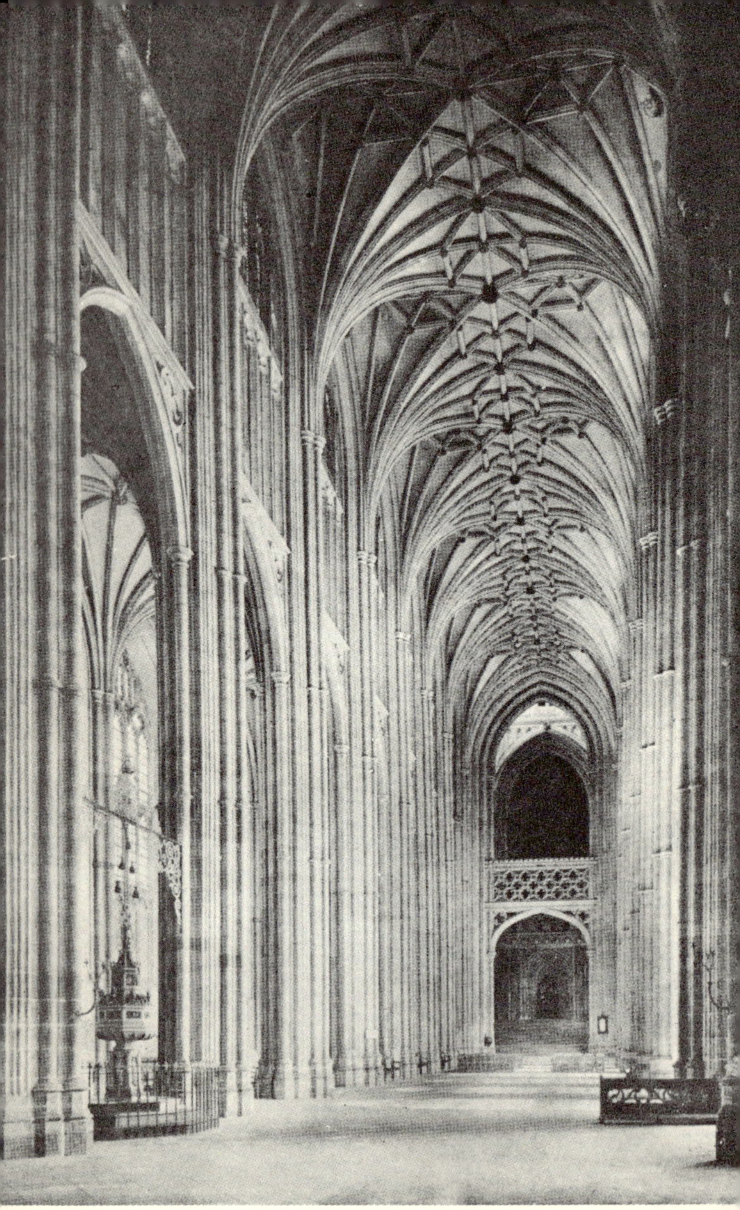

3. Canterbury Cathedral: the Nave

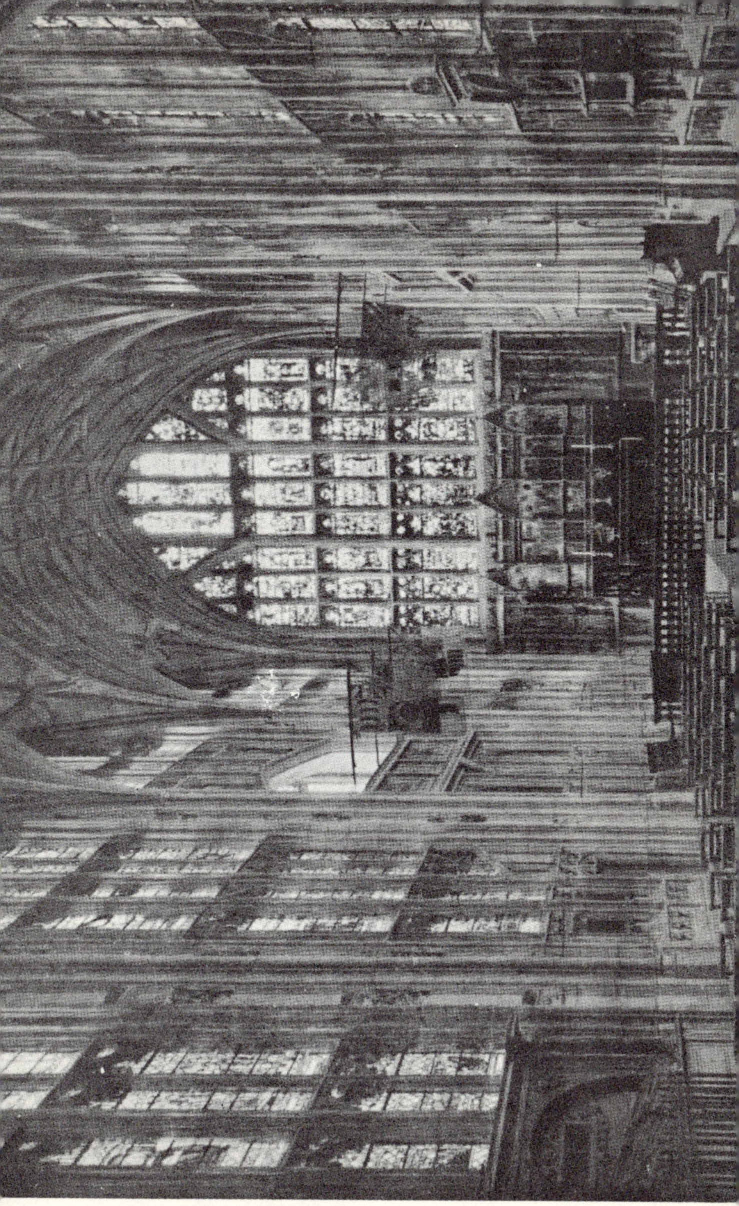

4. Gloucester Cathedral: the East Window

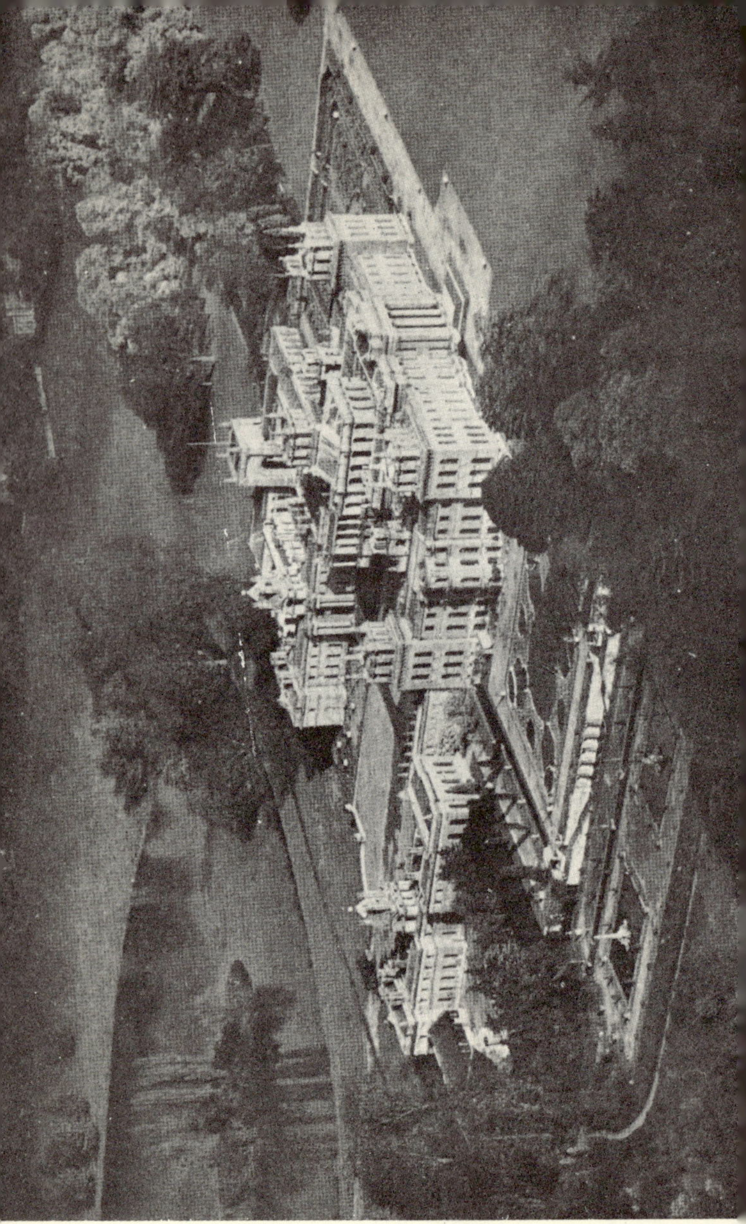

5. Blenheim Palace. Architect: Sir John Vanbrugh. 1705-10

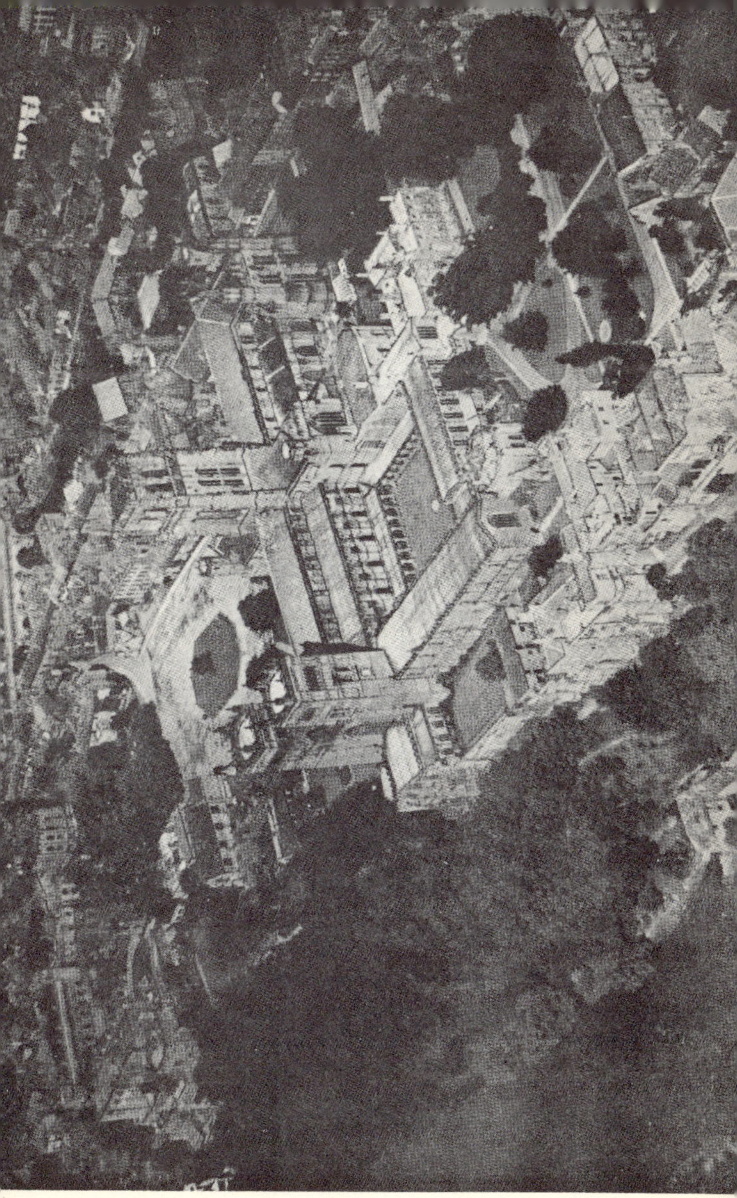

6. Durham Cathedral and Castle

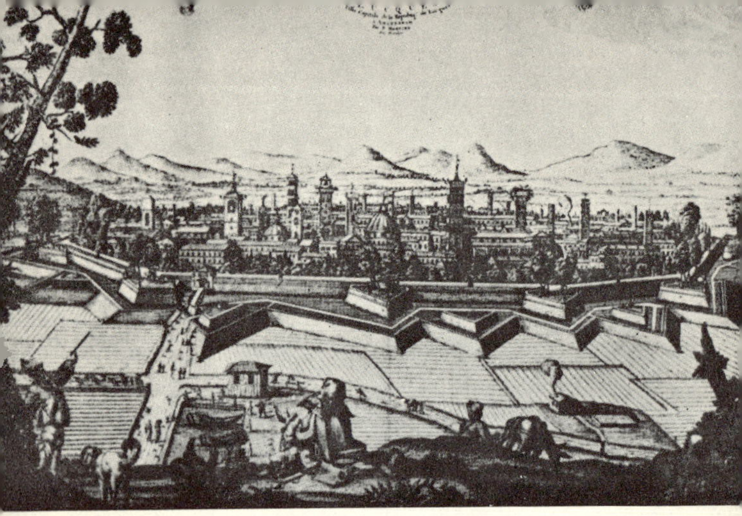

7. (a) A view of Lucca.

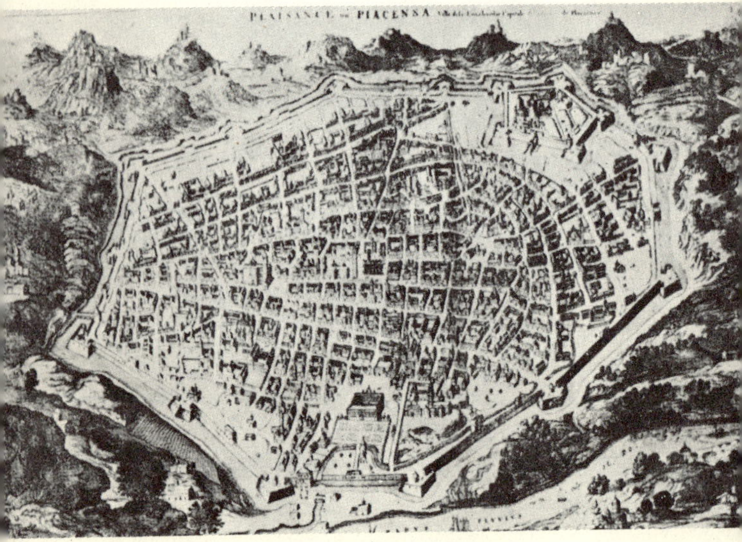

7. (b) A view of Piacenza.
From seventeenth century prints in the collection of Mr. Shepherd Stevens, Yale University

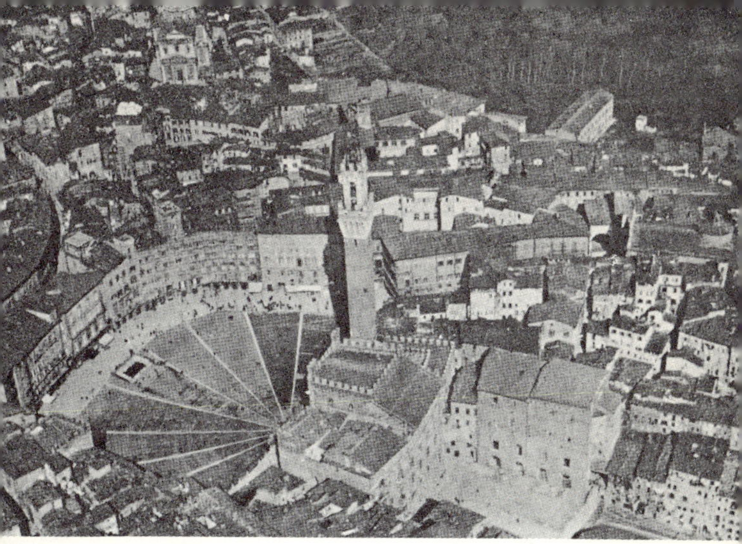

8. (a) Siena: Town Hall and Forecourt

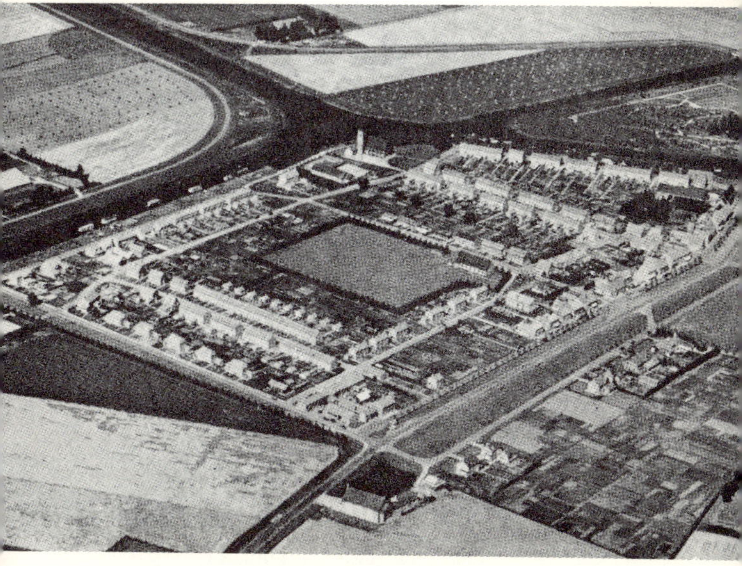

8. (b) View of the town of Wieringerwerf, Holland

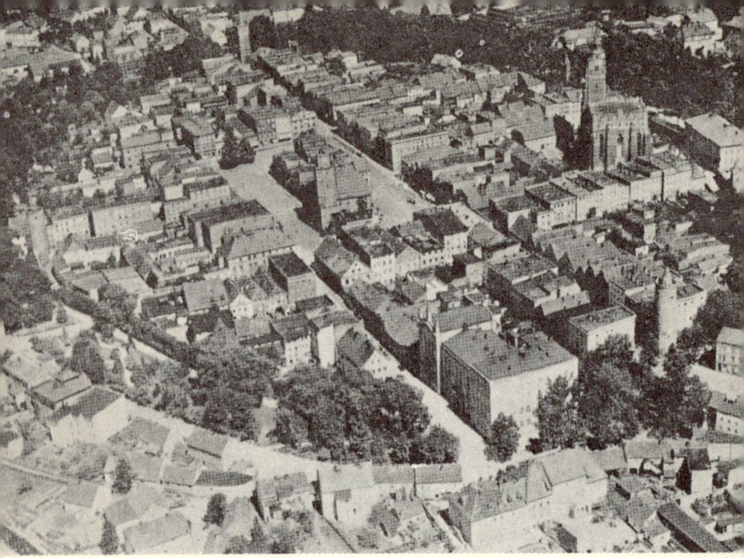

9. (a) Patschkau, Upper Silesia

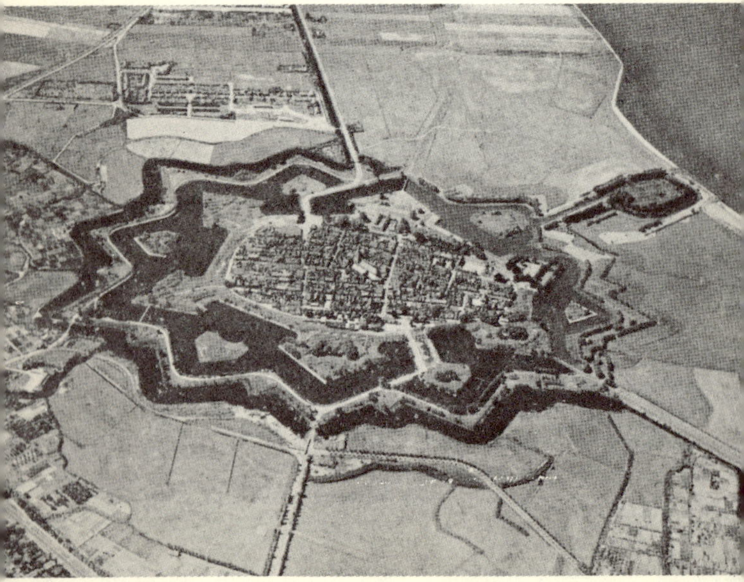

9. (b) Naarden, Holland

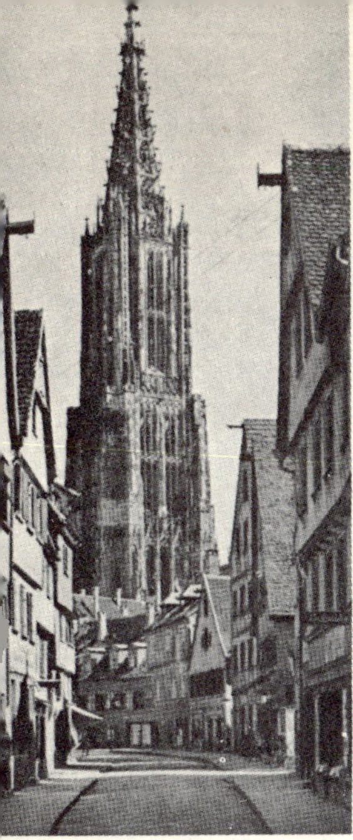

10. (a) Ulm Cathedral,
:n from the Walfischgasse

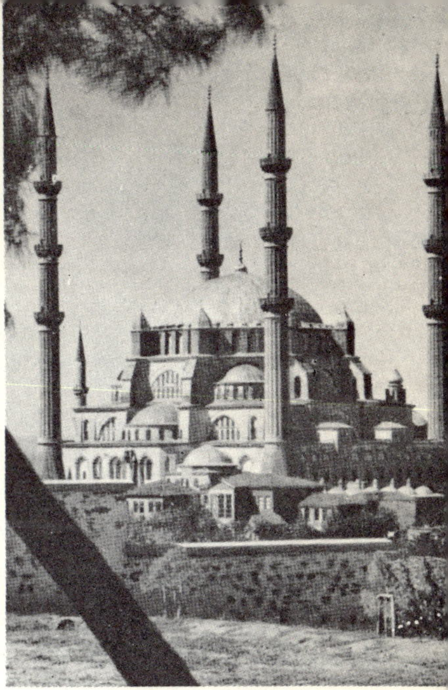

10. (b) The Mosque of Sultan
Selim Camii, Edirne (Turkey)

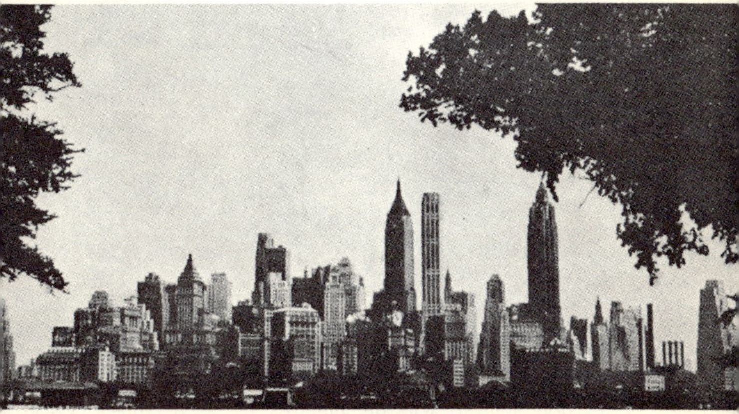

10. (c) Downtown Manhattan from Governor's Island

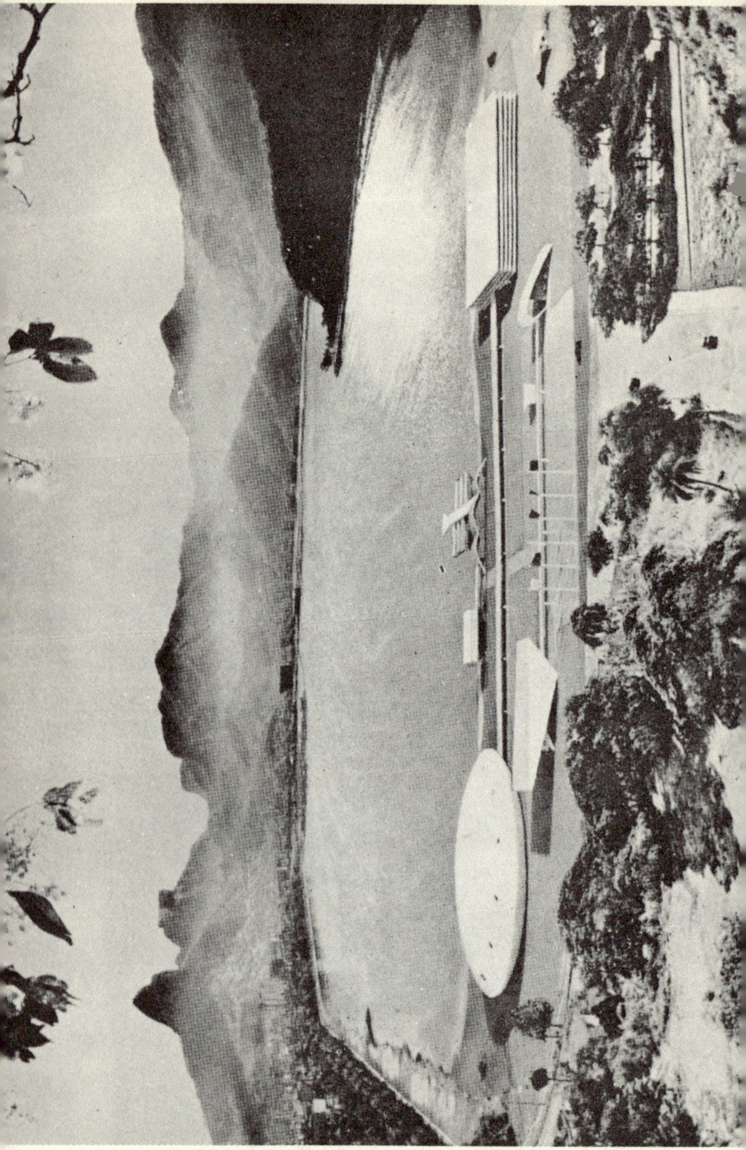

11. Television station, Rio de Janeiro, 1954. Architect: Oscar Niemeyer

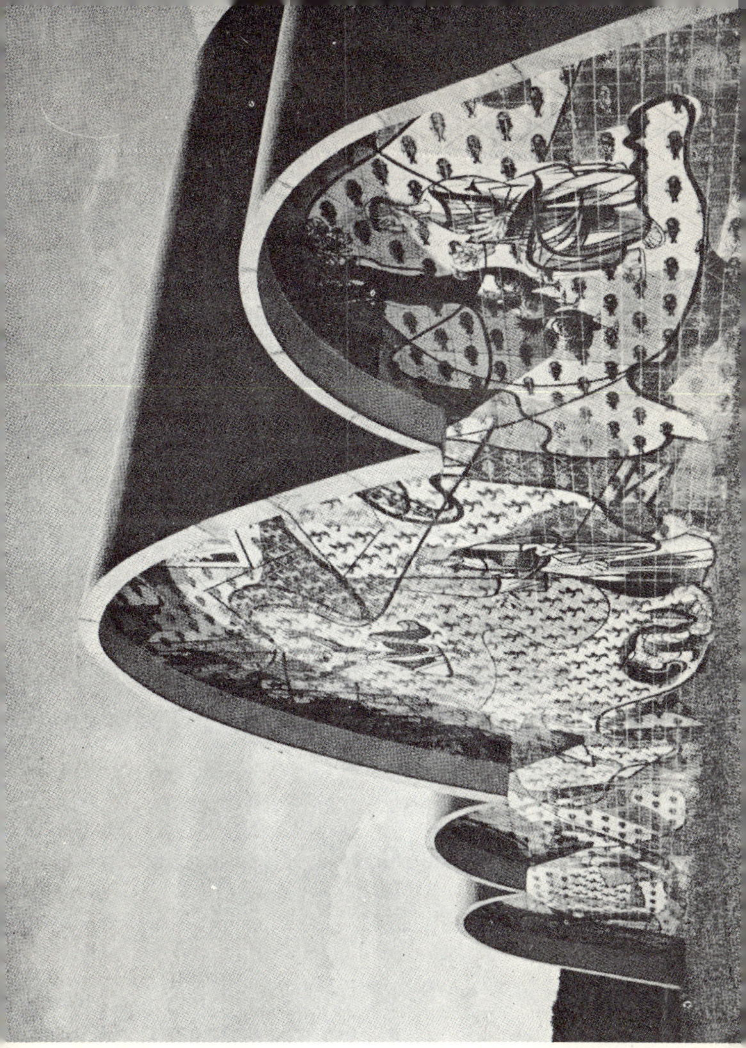

12. Church of Saint Francis of Assisi at Pampulha, Brazil. Architect: Oscar Niemeyer. Structural Engineer: Joaquim Cardozo. The series of vaultings at the rear of the building, with a mural by Portinari, executed in tiles, depicting the life of St. Francis

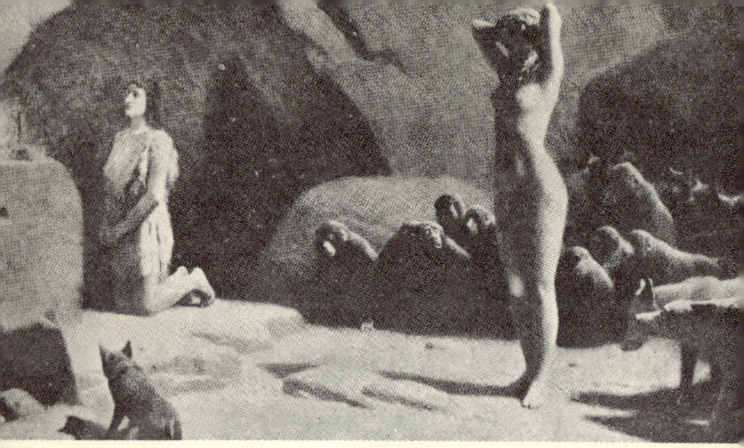

13. Saint Anthony, by John C. Dollman (1851-1934) Royal Academy of Arts, 1897.

"The demons changed themselves into the shapes of beasts and creeping things . . . But when the enemy saw himself to be too weak for Antony's determination, then he attacked him with the temptation he is wont to use"—Gould's Lives of the Saints

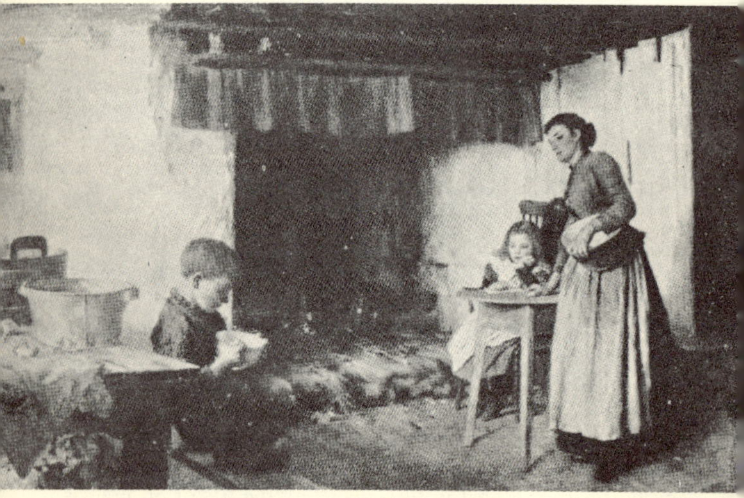

14. "In Faith and Hope the world will disagree, But all mankind's concern is charity."

Painting by Walter Langley (1852-1922) Royal Academy of Arts, 1897

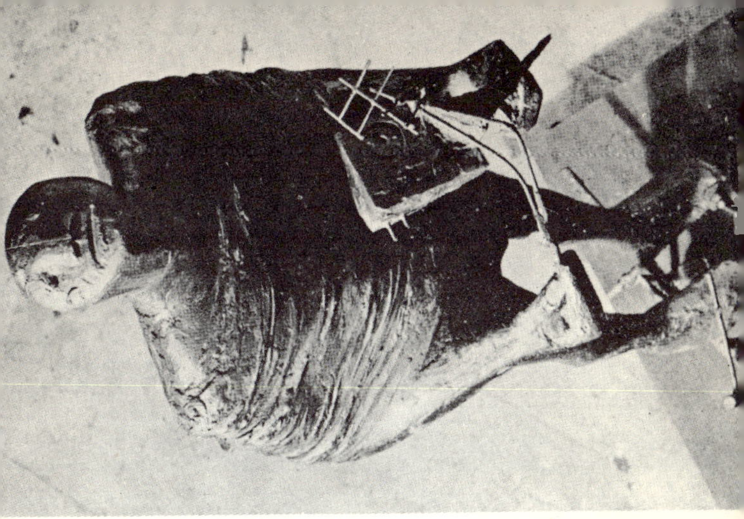

16. The Manipulator. Shell bronze, height 5 ft. 7 in. By Reg Butler, 1945

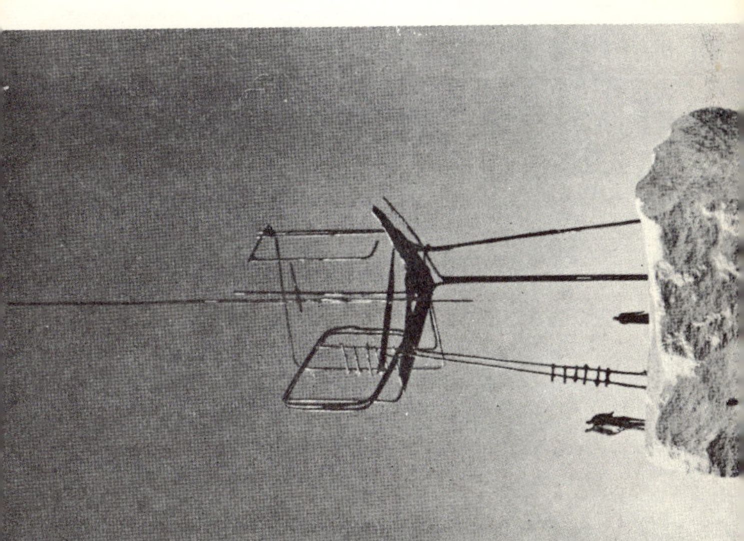

15. Project for a monument to the Unknown Political Prisoner. Prize-Winning design by Reg Butler. 1953

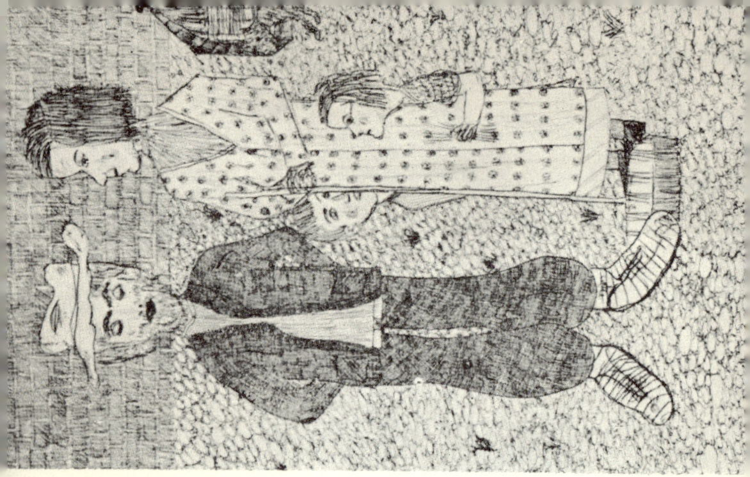

17. (b) "The Family," by a boy of thirteen from an East End school in London.

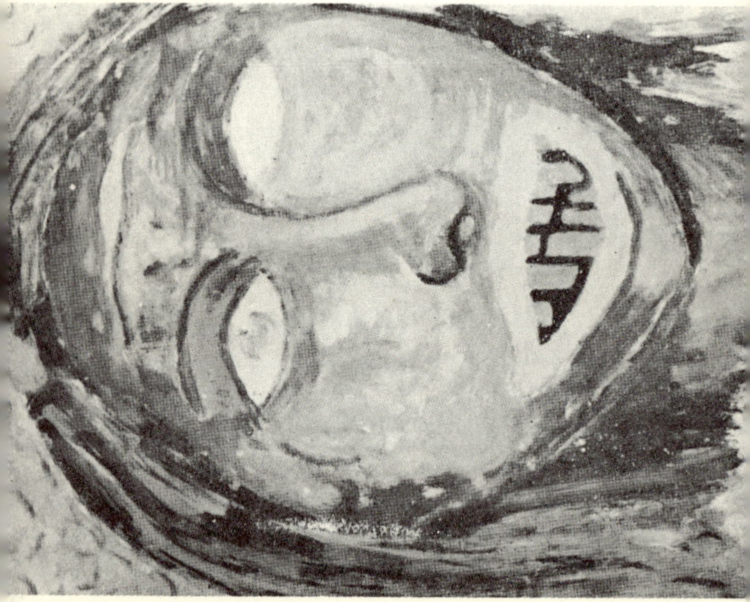

17. (a) "One of the three witches from Macbeth," by a girl of thirteen

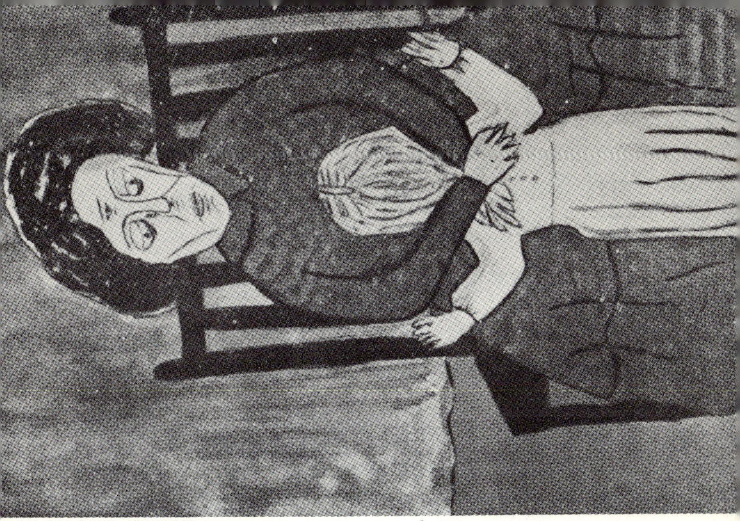

17. (d) "Bedtime Story," by a girl of eleven (L.C.C. school)

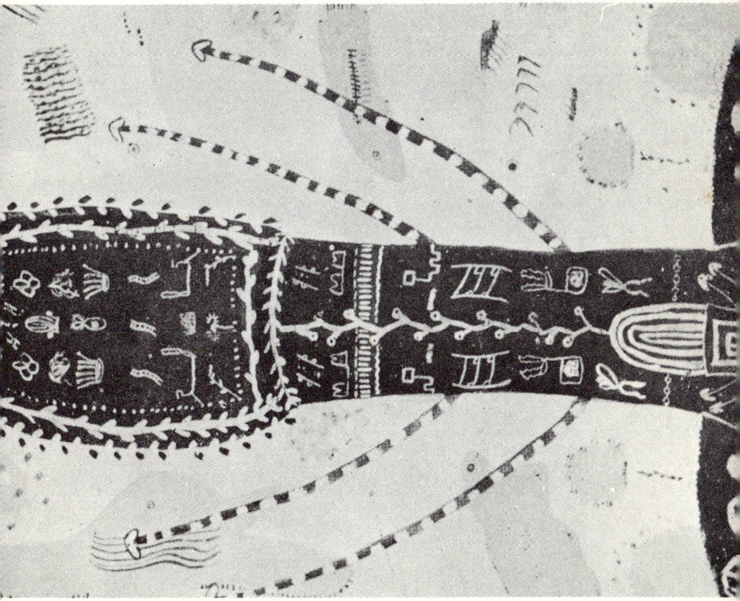

17. (c) "Composition with fish," by a secondary school girl of fourteen

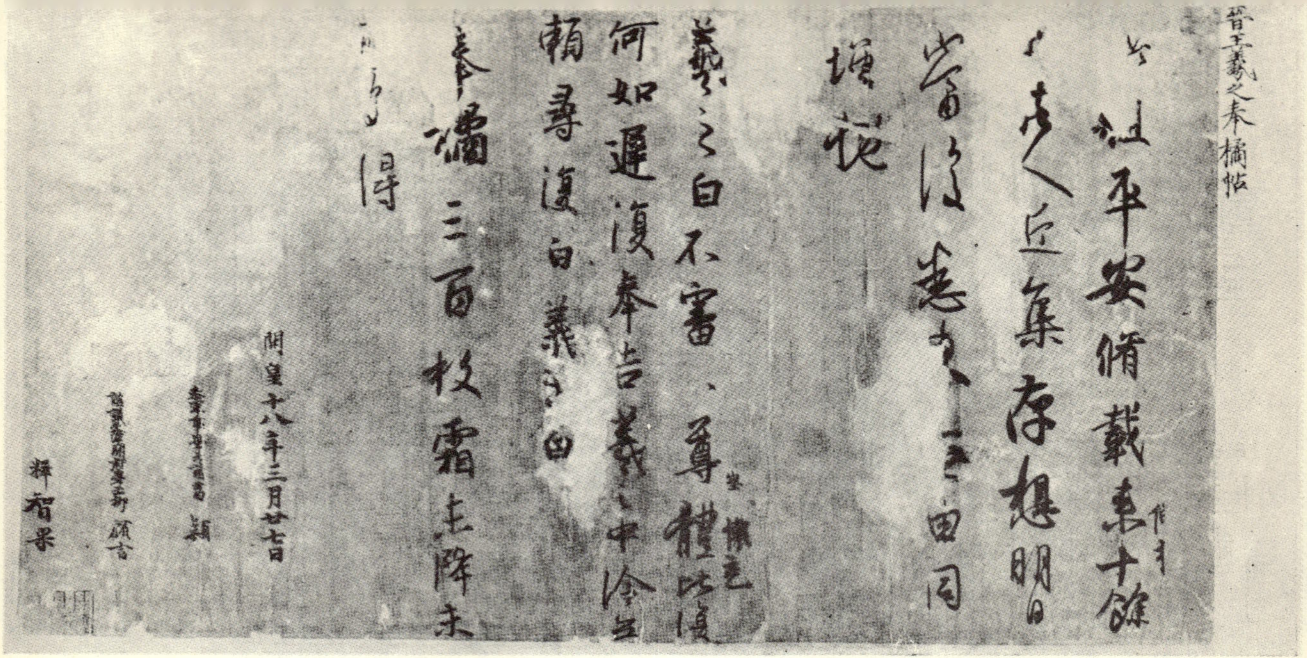

18. The only surviving specimen of Writing by Wang-Hsi-Chih, the most famous of all Chinese calligraphers
(fourth century A.D.)

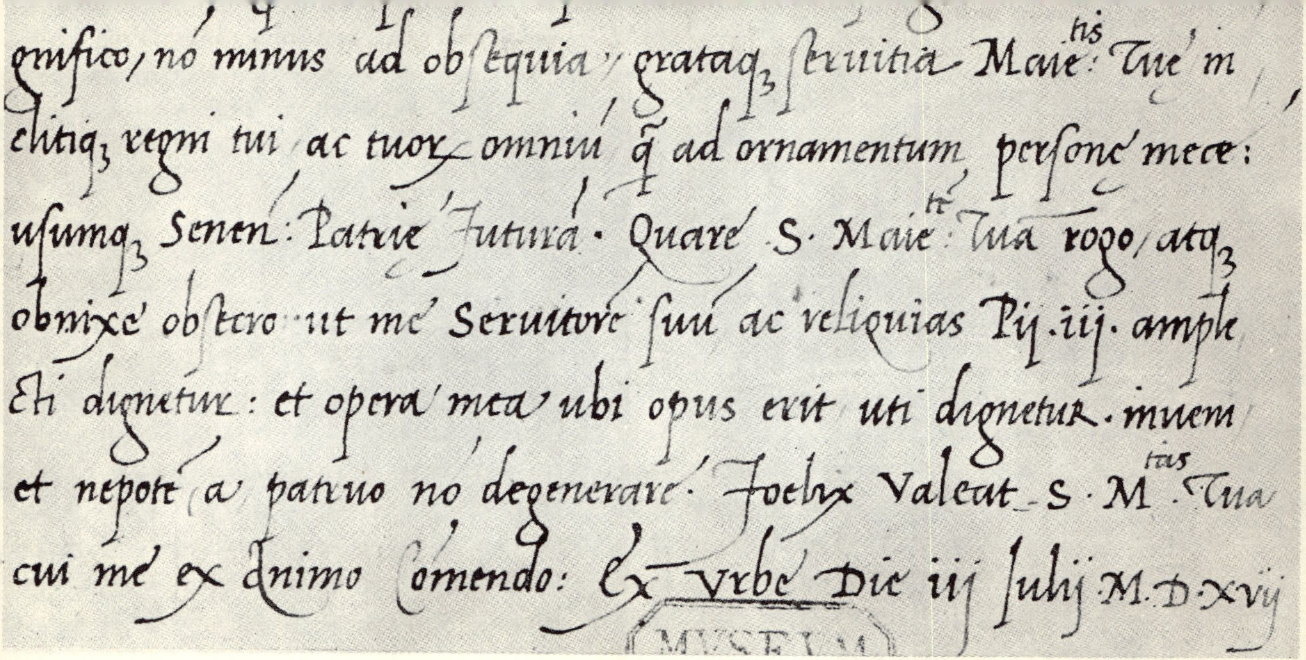
gnifico, no minus ad obsequia, grataq; servitia Maie tis: Tue in
clitiq; regni tui ac tuor omniu q ad ornamentum persone mee:
usumq; Senen: Patrie futura. Quare S. Maie te: Tua rogo, atq;
obnixe obsecro ut me Servitore suu ac reliquias Pij. iij. ample
cti dignetur: et opera mea ubi opus erit uti dignetur. invem
et nepote a patruo no degenerare. Foelix Valeat S. M tas. Tua
cui me ex animo comendo: Ex urbe Die iij Julij M.D.XVij

19. An example of early sixteenth century italic handwriting. From *A Handwriting Manual* by Alfred Fairbank

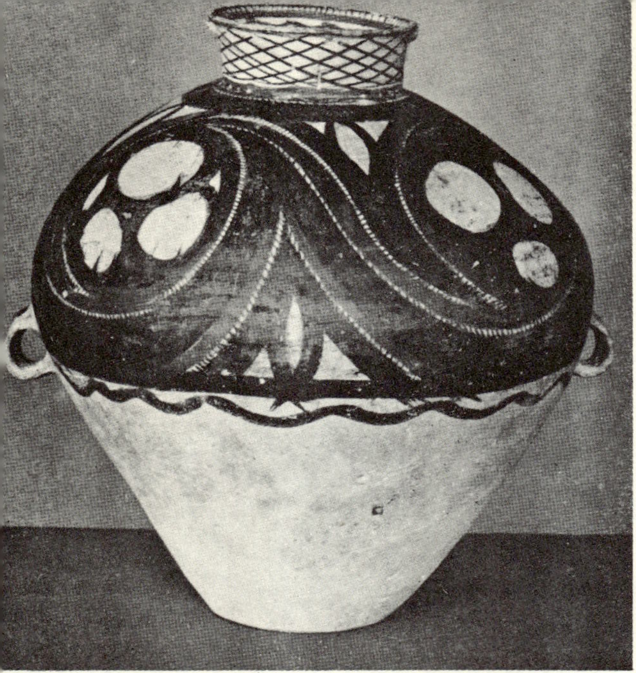

20. (a) Pre-historic vase from Kansu, China

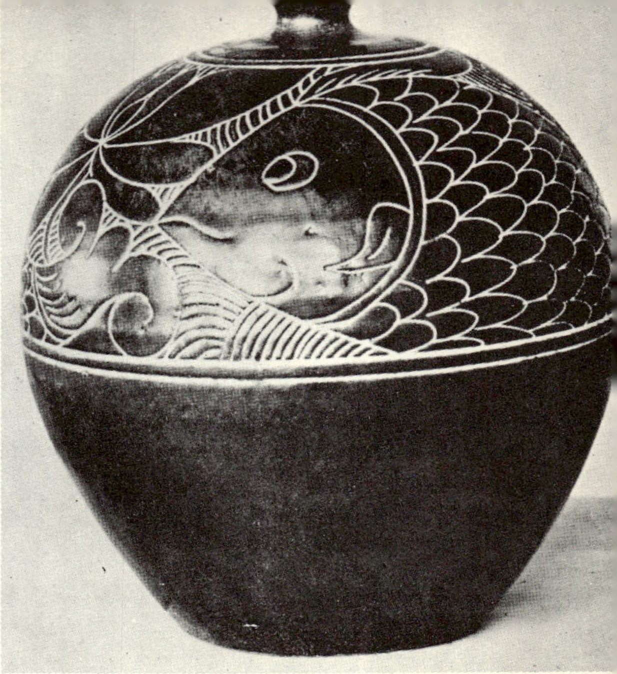

20. (b) Vase with incised decoration (Tz'u Chou type)
Fourteenth century or later

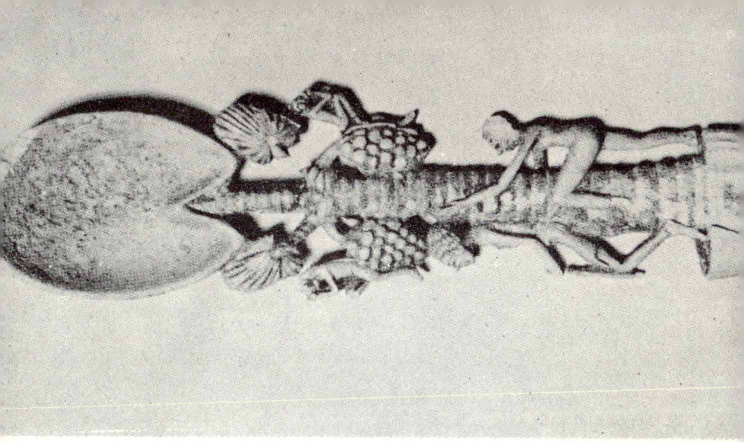

22. Toilet spoon of carved ivory. Egyptian, New Kingdom, Dynasty XVIII (c. 1580-1340 B.C.)

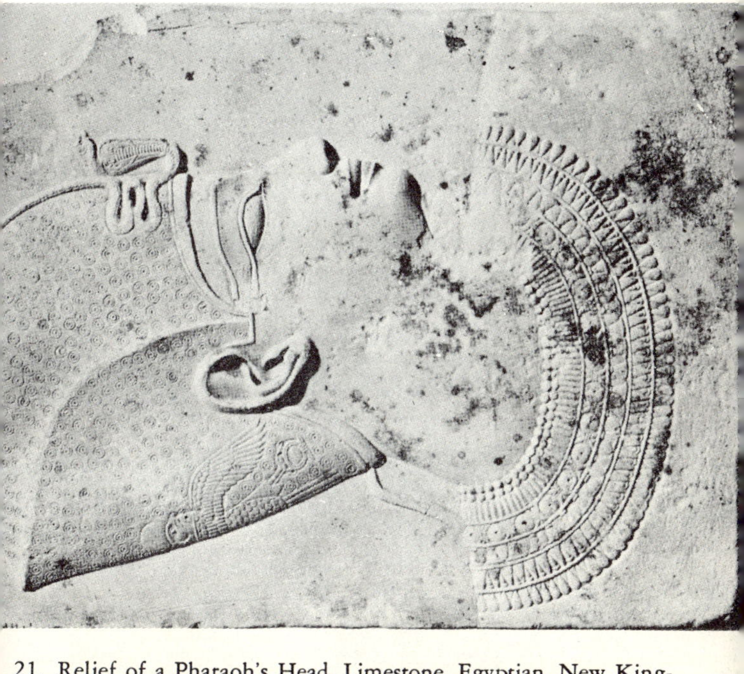

21. Relief of a Pharaoh's Head. Limestone. Egyptian, New Kingdom, Dynasty XVIII (c. 1580-1340 B.C.)

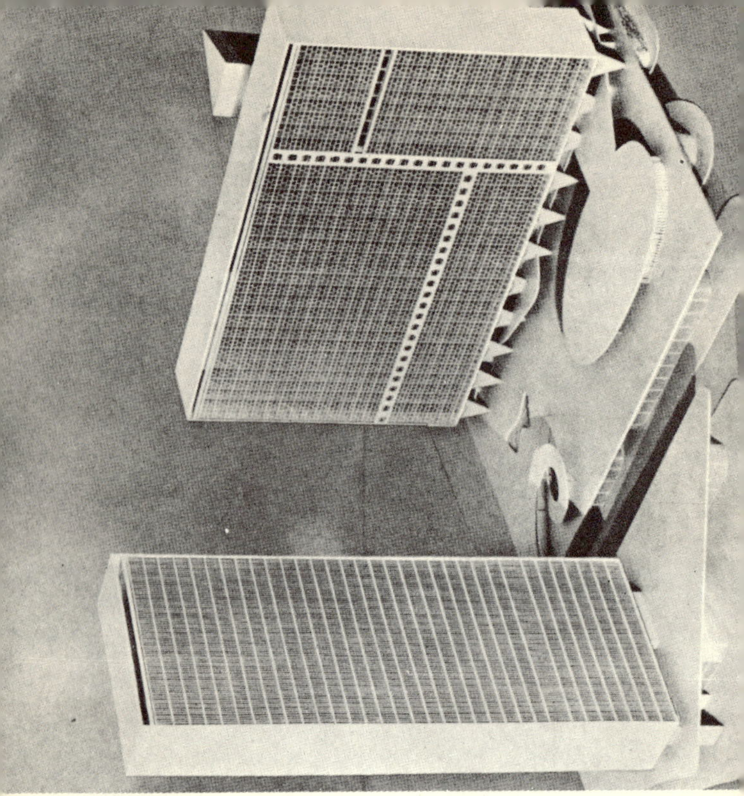

24. Model of the Kubitscheck group of buildings, 1953. In construction. Architect: Oscar Niemeyer

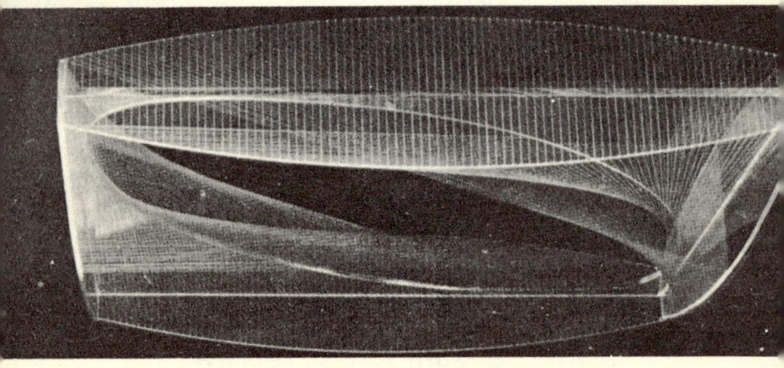

23. Linear Construction, by Naum Gabo. Plastic. 1942-3

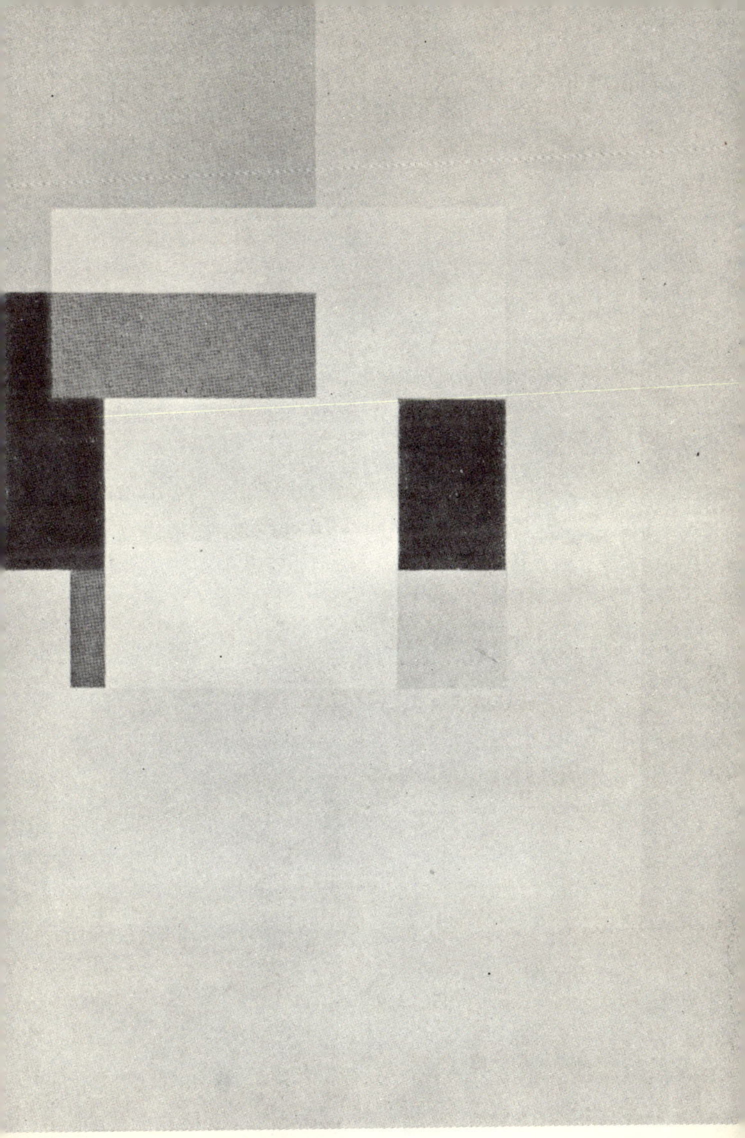

25. Abstract painting by Ben Nicholson, 1937. Collection: J. L. and S. Martin

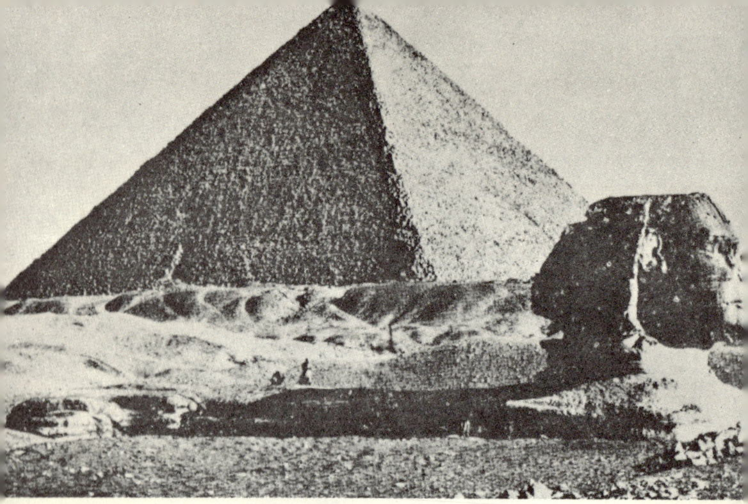

26. Pyramid at Gizeh, Egypt

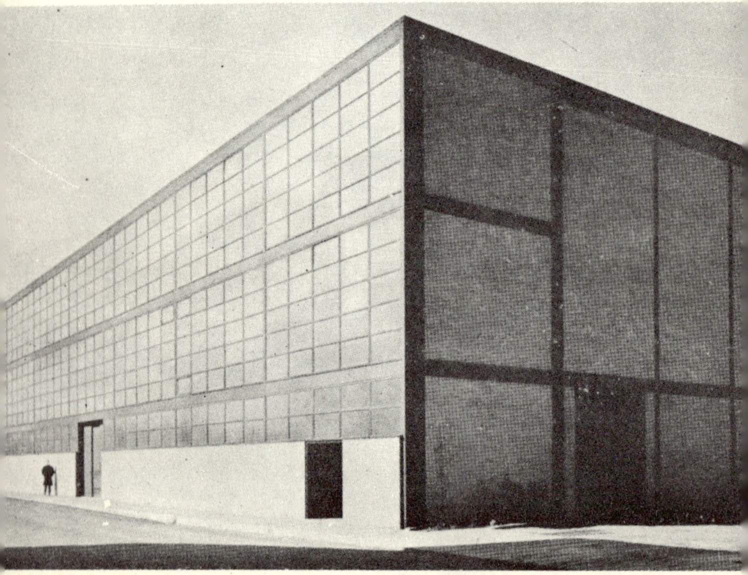

27. Metallurgical Research building, Illinois Institute of Technology, Chicago, 1942-3. Architect: Mies van der Rohe. Holabird and Root, Associated

how you grind it, dissolve it, compress it, it will reform itself at the first opportunity into the same form. The constitution of a crystal can be changed only when chemical changes occur within it.'[1] That truth has been illustrated again and again in the course of history, and very clearly in our own time, in the case of Russia. The only change that permanently affects the structure of society is a chemical change—a change of consciousness, a change of heart. The only question is, how can such a change be effected?

Tolstoy believed that a change of heart, a chemical change in the crystalline structure of society, could be effected only by religion, and by the highest and most perfect form of religion, which is the gospel of Christ, the pure gospel, uncompromised by ecclesiastical authority. *The Kingdom of God is Within You*—that is the title of the work in which he gives his final and greatest message. It is, it seems to me, an immensely optimistic work. It assumes that the spirit of truth is within us, and only awaits a release from the heavy burdens that keep it in subjection—lies, self-deception, hypocrisy and arrogance. Tolstoy seems to assume that in the end a sufficient number of people will see the light apocalyptically: there will be saints of non-resistance who will provide a compelling example to the majority of mankind. But he also believed that art had a decisive rôle to play in the conversion of mankind, and it was perhaps mainly for this reason that he was led to such a narrow view of the nature and functions of art. He thought that the most effective instrument in the establishment of Christianity had been Christ's parables, and he believed that if artists would invent similar parables suitable for the modern man, then art would be fulfilling its real function. This is in all essentials the view of the Communists to-day, but of course they want parables which will be effective in establishing communism. Their theory of the nature and purpose of art is identical with Tolstoy's, but for the Kingdom

[1] *Diaries*, trans. Rose Strunsky (New York, 1917).

of Heaven they substitute whatever is, from year to year, the official version of an earthly paradise.

I believe that art can change the chemical constitution of the social crystal—it is my fundamental belief. But art can only work within its own aesthetic limits. What are such limits? They are, one might say, the limits of the physical universe: they are the laws of proportion and rhythm and harmony which ensure grace and vitality in movement, and beauty in structure—physical, material entities. But physical things—and the human body is a physical thing, and human civilization is a physical thing—can only be changed by physical forces. Spiritual changes will follow on physical changes. It was the belief of Plato, and it is my belief, that the only way in which we can bring about a moral improvement in society is by first effecting an aesthetic improvement. Man is induced to the perceptions of goodness by habits of grace. Beauty of action, beauty of environment, and, above all, the creative experience of beauty, leads inevitably to a sense of nobility, a perfection of character.

It will be said that this belief is as optimistic and as impracticable as Tolstoy's, but there is this fundamental distinction: Tolstoy (and the communists of to-day) begin with mental or psychological entities—feelings, sentiments, beliefs, doctrines—and assume that these can in time change human nature and social institutions. Plato begins with practical activities, geometrical measurements, rhythmical movements—all materialistic elements—and believes that the habitual conditioning of the human body and mind to these can gradually change the human character. I have no doubt which is the more realistic, the more effective policy. But it is a policy which has never been tried. For centuries—throughout the history of the modern world—man has attempted to build new societies on the basis of some religious or political ideal, but always these societies have reverted to patterns of tyranny, of injustice, of crime and suffering. Never once has humanity thought of acting on the assumption that the true basis for moral beauty is plastic beauty.

Such is the secret of the power of all great works of art—the cathartic power of tragedy, the envitalizing power of music, the joy and affirmation that is the colour and form of painting, or the volume and inert power of sculpture. Art is an affirmation, not of reality, but of man's ability to create something beyond reality. Reality, as Sartre has said, is never beautiful. Beauty belongs to the realm of the imagination, and involves a denial of the world as it actually exists. We might say that art is the creation of values by which we judge reality—values that represent all that is positive and expansive, of all that is formative and definitive, of clarity and concentration and unity. Its principles are not moral, are not even spiritual: they are harmonic, and therefore physical. But as such they are paradigms of all intellectual beauty; the patterns of all noble habit. There is no perception of beautiful action—no ideal of equity or love—that is not first evolved in its material perfection in a work of art. Art discovers beauty, for our benefit, for our emulation, for our consolation. All moral impulses, all feelings of goodness, all grace and truth, are but shadows cast from the dance of life: shadows cast, as Shelley said in his great poem, by the light of Intellectual Beauty.

V

The Aesthetic Method of Education

So far, without deliberate intention, the impression created in this book may have been gloomy. The indictment which has been drawn against modern civilization is a severe one, and the material conditions of salvation, when extracted from human history, seem to accord little with the many amenities to which we have become accustomed. My philosophy, however, is not a negative one, and in the remaining two lectures I hope to present you with positive proposals, which, though they entail a revolution in our way of life, are not impossible of achievement if we become urgently aware of the necessity for change.

I have repeatedly drawn attention to *sensibility* as the human quality underlying all processes involving skill, all achievements displaying taste, and I said that the first requirement in any civilization with pretensions to cultural values is a system of education or upbringing which not only preserves the innate sensibility of the child, but makes this the basis of mental development. I now return to that fundamental question.

In all our attempts to define the place of art in society we are continually struggling against the general notion that art is unnatural—that the artist is a rare and eccentric individual, having little or nothing in common with the common man. But it is only greatness that is uncommon, only genius that is eccentric. The appreciation of good form, the perception of rhythm and harmony, the instinct to make things shapely and efficient—these are normal human characteristics, innate rather than acquired, and certainly present in the child from its earliest years. We teach art to children—or perhaps we don't—but what we do not sufficiently realize is that children are artists in any case, just as inevitably as they are walkers or singers, talkers or players of games. Art is merely one method of human expression—the method which makes use of the expressive line, of expressive colour, of plastic form. There is an art of children, just as there is an art of savages or an art of adults. The mistake we make is to assume that this activity in children, the existence of which we can hardly deny, is merely a naive and clumsy attempt to imitate an adult activity. An imitative element is present in all childish activities, but the desire is never to imitate for the sake of imitation, but to communicate something in a common language. The drive behind all such childish efforts is an inner subjective need, not a monkey-like reflex, not an 'aping', as we say, of adult behaviour.

It is very important to admit the truth of this observation, for on such an admission depends the choice between teaching the child to imitate adult standards and recognizing that the child has standards of its own, appropriate to its age and expressive needs and gradually evolving to cope with widening circles of experience. This is a basic distinction in education generally, but for the moment I am only concerned with the effect it has on our attitude towards the aesthetic activity in children.

We are all prepared to admit that art is an affair of the emotions, perhaps also of intuitions and of the intelligence, and we ought therefore to realize that it is not merely a question of the simple growth of a separate faculty, the gradual maturation of a skill. Let us rather consider the analogy of love. The love of a child is one thing, and though the psychoanalysts have taken away our belief in its complete innocence, nevertheless we know that infancy, childhood, adolescence and maturity, represent so many stages in the development of the emotion of love which differ *in kind*. However much we may be deceived by the apparent thread of continuity represented by the uniqueness of each personality, we know that the transition from one stage of emotional development to another is often sudden and cataclysmic. The child of yesterday, attached to its parents by bonds of affection, is suddenly to-day the victim of a passion which makes of it a new being.

The art of the child is the art of a human being with perceptions and emotions, reactions and fantasies, which differ in nature from the perceptions and emotions, reactions and fantasies of the adult. Instead, therefore, of judging the art of children by adult standards, we should be acting more scientifically if we were to compare it with the art of savages and of primitive men generally. Many of the observations which have been made about primitive art can be applied to the art of children. In both cases we are dealing with what Lévy-Bruhl has called *a pre-logical* state of mentality, and the many characteristics which are common to both types of art spring from this fact. The art of children must be studied, not as the child's feeble effort to imitate the plastic modes of expression practised by the civilized adult, but as the child's direct and unsophisticated expression of its own world of feeling. Once we have adopted this correct attitude towards the art of children, once we have an understanding of the place which plastic modes of expression occupy in the child's emotional life, then our methods of teaching children must change radically, and the place which art should occupy in the scheme of education takes on an altogether new significance.

In the researches and experiments which have led to this new understanding of the art of children, no one country can claim pre-eminence. It was Rousseau who first taught us to respect the emotional integrity of the child's world of vision: but Rousseau, from our point of view, is still an intellectualist fully aware of the sensational basis of the child's mode of perception, but using it for rational ends. You will remember that he would have Emile cultivate the art of drawing, but 'not so much for art's sake, as to give him exactness of eye and flexibility of hand'. He would take good care, he said, not to provide Emile with a drawing master, who would only set him to copy copies and to draw from drawings: 'Nature should be his only teacher, and things his only models'. Rousseau specifically excludes drawing from memory, for fear lest his pupil should substitute 'absurd and fantastic forms for the real truth of things, and lose his sense of proportion and his taste for the beauties of nature'.

I think it was Ruskin who first realized that a distinction must be made between drawing from observation, whether of works of art or of nature, and drawing as a spontaneous activity, a form of expression dictated by inner needs, like speech. At any rate, in his *Elements of Drawing*, published in 1857, he suggested that it was 'not advisable to engage a child (under the age of twelve or fourteen) in any but the most voluntary practice of art. If it has a talent for drawing, it will be continually scrawling on what paper it can get; and should be allowed to scrawl at its own free will, due praise being given for every appearance of care, of truth, in its efforts. It should be allowed to amuse itself with cheap colours almost as soon as it has sense enough to wish for them'. These remarks of Ruskin's inspired one of his followers, a teacher called Ebenezer Cooke, to experiment in English schools. Ebenezer Cooke's experiments came to the notice of the leading English psychologist of the period, James Sully, and the result was a book, *Studies of Childhood*, published in 1896, which gave a firm psychological foundation to the study of this activity in children. Meanwhile the subject had been pursued in other countries—by Corrado Ricci in Italy and by Bernard Perez in France. During the past forty years quite an extensive literature has grown up round the subject, in America as well as in Europe, and certain teachers, such as Franz Cizek in Vienna and Marion Richardson in London, have carried out practical experiments in art teaching which have been significant enough to arouse considerable interest in the educational world. I have given a detailed account of this work elsewhere,[1] and here I will only summarize, very briefly and simply, the conclusions that have been derived from the observation of this creative activity in children and the claims that we now make for the practice of a free mode of plastic expression during the course of education.

Let me begin by making clear what we do *not* claim. We do not claim that we are teaching children to observe external objects with exactness. We are not attempting to sharpen the child's powers of observation, of classification, of memory. All that is a pedagogical activity which we are content to leave to the science master, and we would agree that a certain type of drawing or design should be taught, like writing and numeration, in conjunction with scientific observation: it is a necessary form of notation or record. It is a skill which becomes appropriate at the secondary stage of education.

In the second place—and it is most important to appreciate this point—we are *not* attempting to create professional artists. To become a competent painter or sculptor in the professional sense will require a long and arduous training in technique, and this vocational instruction should be given (as it is at present) in institutions specially devoted to the purpose. We teach children to speak, but we do not expect them all to be orators: we teach them to write, but we do not expect them all to be poets. In the same way, we

[1] *Education Through Art* (London, 1944).

teach them to draw and paint and model without any expectation that art will necessarily become their exclusive vocation in life.

What we do teach children by all these means is a particular medium of expression. Sounds, words, lines, colours—all these are the raw materials out of which the child has to learn to communicate with the outer world. He has also at his command certain gestures, which he combines with sounds, words, lines and colours. In his difficulty—for it is enormously difficult at first for the child to make himself understood—he will use everything that comes to hand: he makes a total effort to express himself, to express his inner feelings and desires.

Normally the parent and teacher make every effort to understand the *verbal* signs which the child makes: we listen to the first babblings of the baby and try to construe them into words. How patiently we guide and encourage the child in his efforts, first to talk and then to write!

But the child has also at his command this other language of line and colour, and he could often say by this means things for which he still lacks the words. He can express his emotions and desires, his perceptions and daydreams, by signs and symbols, by approximate representations. But more often than not his efforts in this direction receive no encouragement from the teacher, and even less from the parent. This activity, which should flourish as naturally as speech, is discouraged and becomes atrophied. The child is then visually dumb, a word which originally meant stupid.

But if we do not encourage the child to develop his visual communications, his language of images, a new direction for expansion and growth is opened up for him. We might say that one of our aims, and perhaps the chief one, should be to give the child the necessary confidence and skill to develop a new but quite natural medium of expression—to make the language of symbols as much a trained habit as the language of signs, to give the pictograph the same significance as the phonetic alphabet. But our secondary aim is to encourage the child to reveal its personality, its innate characteristics. For the parent and the teacher a child's drawings become a new window into the child's mind.

But there is more to be discovered than the psychology of the individual child. As we gather and correlate this plastic imagery produced by children, we learn much about children in general, about their common characteristics and their mental development. And finally, but not in my opinion least important, we learn much about the nature of the aesthetic activity, about the place of art in life and in the evolution of mankind. For what these children produce is not merely line and colour, but line and colour (form, too, and cubic volume) which are significant and expressive, and which are significant and expressive quite naturally and instinctively. We learn, in short, that the primary elements of art—the factors which make it emotionally effective—are given to it by man's own nature and needs, and are not the creation of man's consciousness and intellect (Figs. 17 *a–d*).

It would be wrong to give the impression that the aesthetic method in education is generally accepted in English schools. Such experiments are not part of an official policy, though they have the sympathy of many directors of education. It should be realized that the English educational system is still to a large extent decentralized. There is a central authority, the Ministry of Education, but there are also the numerous Local Education Authorities, and these preserve a large measure of autonomy. And then we have our so-called 'public' schools, which are very private and exclusive, and numerous schools of a more or less independent character, run by religious communities or even by private individuals. This loose structure permits a degree of experiment which would not be possible under a rigidly totalitarian system. I do not want to suggest that experiments are confined to schools of a more or less private character: on the contrary, some of the most interesting experimental work has taken place under authorities such as the London County Council, and anywhere one might find an enterprising director of education willing and able to try out new ideas in the schools under his control. The type of work illustrated in the accompanying plate comes from no particular type of school, nor from the children of any particular class of society. It comes from elementary schools in the East End of London and from fashionable private schools, from secondary schools and schools for epileptic children. One thing that has been demonstrated beyond any doubt is that the aesthetic faculty is present in every child as a birthright, and that it can be made to blossom in the most unlikely surroundings—in gloomy industrial slums no less than in the beautiful precincts of a school like Eton or Winchester. Of course, as the child grows and its perceptions feed more or less consciously on its environment, this environment begins to be reflected in the subject matter of the child's art. But only in the subject matter. The style can develop independently of the content. It is not the environment which matters so much as the method of teaching.

If you now ask me: What is this method of teaching practised in schools which produce the paintings I have shown, my answer can only be in the most general terms. I am not myself a teacher, and I do not like to dictate to those who carry on this most difficult vocation. But I observe teachers and I note the results: I see that certain methods lead to results which I consider good, other methods to results which I consider bad, or to no results at all. It is easier to describe the methods which have bad results than those which have good results, for the former are definite and decisive, the latter infinitely subtle and uncertain. The bad results are always produced by a method which is too conscious and deliberate, by a discipline which is imposed from without, which is the command of a drill-sergeant. The good results are produced apparently by no method at all, or by a system of hints and suggestions, and the discipline which undoubtedly exists and *must* exist, arises out of the activity itself, is in fact a kind of concentration on tools and materials, an absorption in concrete things. The good teacher is not a dictator, but rather a pupil more advanced in technique than the others, more conscious of the aim to be achieved and the means that must be adopted, who works with the children, sympathizes with them and encourages them, gives them that priceless possession which is self-confidence. It is only fear that prevents the child from being an artist—fear that its private world of fantasy will seem ridiculous to the adult, fear that its expressive signs and symbols will not be adequate. Cast out fear from the child, and you have then released all its potentialities for emotional growth and maturation.

That, of course, is not the final stage of education. You have liberated the child from fear, but beyond liberation there must be the more positive world of co-operation. You have liberated the child by means of sympathy and understanding, and the same faculties must be used to create human bonds, social bonds, until the individual child finds his fulfilment in the adult world of the community. That is the general purpose of education, but I know of no methods so effective for this purpose as those which are in a concrete sense *creative*. As individuals we create to communicate: we create a language out of sounds, we create a pictorial language out of line and colour. But every language, even the language of art is a communal creation; it represents an agreed system of signs, to be used in common. Art is a bond. It is not a bond which should be the exclusive privilege of a class, of a tiny group of connoisseurs and artists. Art should be an integral part of our communal life, as it was in Ancient Greece, as it was in the Middle Ages: and it should enter our lives at their formative stage, as a natural function of human relationships, as the language of form and colour, as universal and as innocent as the language of words.

It may be objected that when I speak of the language of form and colour, I am confining myself to a much narrower conception of art than was prevalent in Ancient Greece or in the Middle Ages. In all our discussions of the place of art in education, there is admittedly a tendency to confine our observations to pictorial art. We think of art as predominantly visual, and we seem to ignore those other modes of expression, whether of speech or of sound, which are also forms of art of equal importance. By confining my observations in this lecture to children's drawings, I may seem to be guilty of the same neglect, not only of music and poetry, but even of sculpture and architecture. Let me therefore make it perfectly clear to you that anything I have to say about the art of children, and its importance in education, applies to all the arts. At the same time I think there is something more than mere convenience in the preference we give in this matter to pictorial art. Plato betrayed a similar partiality for the art of music, and nearly all his illustrations were drawn from that art. Again, I don't think it was merely a question of convenience for Plato. We choose the illustrations which are most apt—that is to say, we resort to the art which the civilization we live in finds most utilitarian. Music, in Plato's time, was the normal adjunct to the religious festivals and public entertainments in which the Athenian public indulged: it was the accompaniment to their daily life. We cannot say the same of music nowadays: it is still there, in the background, especially if our neighbour leaves his radio on all day. But in modern life music is a subordinate art and does not compare, in the range and power of its appeal, to the stream of pictorial images which passes into the public consciousness through the channels of the press, the cinema, advertisements and illustrated books. The eye, perhaps, has a certain priority among our organs of sensation. I am not giving pictorial art more importance for this reason: I am merely defending the convenient use we make, and should make, of the pictorial image as a means of propaganda: even as a means of education. But the means is not the end: the end is the development of a balanced aesthetic awareness which is expressed in all media—not only in painting, but also in sculpture, weaving, embroidery, music, dancing, poetry and drama.

There is one further point to note: art is a natural discipline. In an obvious sense, art is a discipline imposed by the tool and the material—a child cannot use a pencil or a pen, a brush or a potter's wheel, without discovering that in order to be expressive, hand and eye must work in an instinctive unison. Art in this way produces an integration of the senses which we call *skill*, and which is one of the most fundamental purposes of any system of education, as I pointed out in my first lecture. But art is also a discipline in another and a more profound sense. There is in the very process of perception, and in this complementary process of expression, an instinctive tendency to *form*. The formal perfection of most primitive works of art, achieved without any system of instruction, has often been a subject for wonder and astonishment. The unsophisticated art of children, before any instruction is given, has the same tendency towards formal organization—not only balance of composition and selective emphasis of significant detail, but also towards expressive line and harmonious colour. Natural expression has its own instinctive form, and this would seem to suggest that the aim of education should be to seize on this innate sense of discipline, in order to develop and mature it, rather than to impose on the child a system of discipline which may be alien to its nature and harmful to its mental growth.

When the mental growth of the child has been impeded, and its psyche distorted (with results which are definitely neurotic and even delinquent), then there is much evidence which suggests that the practice of a creative art may have a therapeutic effect, gradually leading the child back to a balanced psychological disposition. The wider claims which are made for the place of art in education do not stop short at the achievement of a balanced personality for each individual child: that integration of the personality which is aimed at is an integration within the group or community to which the child belongs. We have never dared to trace the connections between the disordered state of our civilization and our traditional systems of education. If our schools were producing naturally and normally personalities which we could describe as balanced, integrated or harmonious, we should not be able to tolerate a condition of universal disunity and mutual distrust. We should therefore re-examine our whole tradition of education since the Renaissance and dare to ask ourselves whether it has been generally productive of individual serenity and social harmony. We might then have to confess that in our exclusive preoccupation with knowledge and science, we had omitted to educate those human faculties which are connected with the emotional and integrative aspects of human life—that we had carefully nurtured inhuman monsters, with certain organs of the intelligence gigantically enlarged, others completely atrophied. I am not making scientific assertions: I am merely pointing out that in certain directions we have not dared to question the presuppositions of our academic traditions and that at the same time these presuppositions have a clear connection with the character of our civilization.

I hope I have now made it clear that what I have called the development of a balanced aesthetic awareness is not an end in itself. Our aim is the same as Plato's—the moral and intellectual wholeness or health of mankind—and art is for me, as it was for Plato, a means to this end. But that has not been the general purpose of education since the Renaissance. I think one might go so far as to say that since the rise of scholasticism in the Middle Ages, education has taken many forms, but essentially, during all these centuries, its aim has been to increase the powers of the intellect, to discipline the emotions and to build up a knowledge and understanding of the natural world. That aim has been pursued with such consistency and singleness of mind that, according to some anatomists, the very structure of the human brain has been altered and physiological tensions have been set up which are definitely perceptible as processess alien to the organisms as a whole.[1] I am not capable of handling the evidence, but I think it is worth noting in passing that there is some biological evidence for the belief (or rather, since it is contrary to the common belief, the heresy) that human nature can be changed.

Those people, the majority, who believe that human nature cannot be changed, usually make this dogma a basis for their further belief that we shall never abolish war.Man is a fighting animal, they say, and since there is no possibility of changing his nature, he will continue to fight until, presumably, the human race, like the Kilkenny cats, is no more. This is, of course, a very illogical and unscientific point of view. We know that some human beings are aggressive and others unaggressive: that some communities are martial in spirit, others pacific. We now have a hypothesis—the so-called frustration-aggression hypothesis—which offers a comprehensive explanation of this duplicity in human nature. Aggression, it asserts, is always a consequence of frustration. Avoid frustration and we shall thereby eliminate the psychological basis of war and all other forms of aggression.[2]

It seems to come to this: we could change human nature if we could avoid the frustration of certain instinctual drives which are part of the inherited characteristics of each human being. I do not

[1] Cf. Trigant Burrow, *Biology of Human Conflict* (New York, 1937), p. 117.

[2] Cf. John Dollard and others, *Frustration and Aggression*, Institute of Human Relations, Yale University (New Haven, 1937).

wish on the present occasion to spend any time discussing the nature of these instincts: we are all aware of their existence, and we know that their perversion results in the formation of what we call 'bad habits'. Education, from this point of view, is the teaching of 'good habits'—but how do innate instinctual drives, which are presumably in their origin ethically neutral, or merely egotistical, become 'good' habits rather than 'bad' habits? That, as Plato and Aristotle recognized long ago, is the crux of the educational problem, and it is still a problem, which, in spite of Plato and Aristotle and all the educational philosophers who followed them, remains unsolved.

It remains unsolved in practice, but not, I think, in theory. The theory was formulated at the beginning, by Plato and Aristotle, but that theory has never yet been put into practice. We might go so far as to say that the theory has never yet been taken seriously. Why?

To restate the theory is to risk the displeasure of all those who have had their grounding in these classical commonplaces. But in statements and restatements, everything depends on the emphasis given to particular aspects of a theory, and it is a wrong emphasis which in this particular case has been responsible for an age-long misunderstanding.

The theory begins with a clear distinction between *moral* and *intellectual* virtue. I need not elaborate the distinction, but please observe that once two things have been separated, it is possible henceforth to treat them separately—to hand over the teaching of moral virtue to one institution and the teaching of intellectual virtue to another. That is, in effect, what happened at the Renaissance: the teaching of moral virtue became the exclusive concern of the Church, the teaching of intellectual virtue the exclusive concern of the State. The Church has never pretended to teach moral virtue on Platonic lines, so the fact that the Church has failed to carry out its assignment is merely what a Platonist would expect. What is important to emphasize is that the State (in which term I include all secular institutions permitted or authorized to act in the name of the State), relieved of the necessity of inculcating moral virtue, was able to concentrate on that immense development of rational thought which has culminated in the atomic bomb. So overwhelming was the progress in this direction that intellectual values began, in the seventeenth century if not earlier, to invade the province of moral education, until we arrive at the paradoxical situation in which even ethics is held to be a *science*, subject to quantitative laws.[1]

Leaving on one side intellectual virtue, the development of which may or may not be justified by the immense structure of modern philosophy and science, we should direct our attention to the fate of moral virtue, which Plato and Aristotle regarded not merely as of equal importance, but even as having a certain priority in education. These Greek philosophers said again and again that all the intellectual virtue man is capable of is not only useless, but indeed dangerous, unless it is grafted on to a stock of moral goodness. By ignoring the essential priority of moral virtue, our systems of education are merely putting dangerous instruments into the hands of people whose instinctual life may be, not merely unformed, but even evilly disposed.

The only method of moral education developed in the modern world is education by precept. These are the laws, these are the commandments, this is done and that is not done by the best people: obey, conform, go and do likewise. If we could assume that these laws and commandments were perfect, ordained by God, and not the mere accumulation of customs and superstitions, there might be some virtue in such a system. We know that human beings are very apt to learn by imitation, especially social imitation.

[1] Cf. C. H. Waddington, *The Scientific Attitude* (London, 1942).

But if they are imitating an imperfect pattern, no improvement takes place. We merely propagate one another's vices, along with a few convenient virtues. For this reason we must look outside human society for the pattern of moral virtue, and the only pattern outside ourselves is our environment, in so far as that is enduring. Look into the structure of the physical universe: there, said Plato and Aristotle, you will find the pattern of moral virtue. Repeat that pattern in your lives, impress it on your souls, do this habitually and especially in childhood, and then goodness will become second nature to you.

Plato did not put forward this theory as a likely hypothesis: he attempted to give it a logical demonstration. It was already evident to the Greeks that certain laws are exhibited in the structure of the physical universe: laws of harmony and proportion, of balance and rhythm. Modern physics has, of course, enormously reinforced the early perceptions of Greek science in this respect. The same laws, Plato was quick to perceive, are also exhibited in the most perfect and efficient forms of human activity: in music, in dancing, in gymnastics, in the rhythms of poetry and the harmonies of painting or sculpture. The inference was then simple enough—so simple that for twenty-four centuries it has seemed too bold and revolutionary. Make the rhythmic arts the basis of your methods of education, said Plato. Then, quite naturally, quite inevitably, you instil into children that sense of form or grace which is the foundation of moral goodness. That is the theory, simple and inflexible, which Plato taught in the *Laws* no less eloquently than in the *Republic*. It is simple, it is clear: the only mystery is why the world has for so long neglected it.[1]

There are many possible explanations of this mystery. To the Christian world of the Middle Ages, in so far as it was known to

[1] Recently it has been brilliantly restated by Hans Kayser, in *Akróasis, die Lehre von der Harmonie der Welt* (Basle, 1946).

them, such a theory must have seemed pagan, humanistic, without divine sanction. More difficult to explain is the failure of the Renaissance to revive the theory with any sense of actuality. It is true that the theory was rediscovered and restated—by Alberti, for example. But by then moral education had become hopelessly confused with religious instruction, and this confusion was to be deepened by the Reformation. With the growth of puritanism an immense paradox was foisted on the world: the supposed antagonism of art and religion, of grace and goodness. In England, and in the United States, we still live within the limits of that moral blackout.

In general, two great mental changes are necessary before we can hope to give Plato's theory of education a trial: a return to the Platonic ideal of moral virtue, which involves what we call 'a change of heart'; and a true appreciation of the significance of the creative activity. The change of heart may be forced upon us by our desperate straits—it is the wider problem of the crisis of our civilization. But one change is implicated in the other, and I have failed if I have not persuaded you that a true appreciation of the creative activity is the best hope of a solution of our moral crisis. The means by which we can achieve the moral revolution are themselves the substance of an enduring culture.

VI

The Decentralization of Art

The decentralization of art is part of a larger problem of the widest sociological scope, and if we are to consider it as a separate subject, it can only be because our special interests, or our special qualifications, justify a partial approach to a common task. In the end we must join hands with the economists and sociologists, and with political philosophy in general. The condition of disease or devitalization which affects all the arts of the world today is but one aspect of that condition of disease or devitalization which shows its most obvious symptoms in social unrest, economic crises and war. At the same time, we must insist that this world-wide disintegration is more than economic, and even economists are beginning to realize, as one of them has said, that 'the boundless over-evaluation of economics is one of the symptoms of the disease of the nineteenth century'. It must be recognized, says this same economist, 'that even within the economic sphere itself the vital and anthropological aspects which cannot be measured are more important than the essentially economic one which can. . . . Economics is merely a means, the "vital situation", the end'.[1]

[1] Alexander Rüstow, Appendix to *International Economic Disintegration*, by Wilhelm Röpke (Hodge, London, 1942).

Explaining what he means by the 'vital situation', Professor Rüstow mentions 'artificial existence in big cities which are so far removed from nature . . . the decay of the family . . . life in the slums . . . conditions in factories where workers are herded together . . . the mechanical specialization of their work . . . the speed of mass-production and . . . the equal tempo and bewildering futility of the amusement and diversion of big city life'. In the same volume from which I quote, Professor Röpke speaks of 'the challenging problem of the proletariat, which, in the last resort, is a human (vital) rather than an economic one. We are today tending more and more to realize that the real cause of the discontent of the working classes is to be sought in the devitalization of their existence, so that neither higher wages nor better cinemas can cure it. To be herded together in giant factories like sheep or soldiers; to devote the vitally important hours of life to work under heteronomous regimentation and without fully realizing the sense and dignity of individual labour; to be uprooted from all natural bonds; to return to gloomy slums and to seek recreation in amusements as senseless, mechanized and devitalized as their work itself; to be dependent every minute of the day on the anonymous forces of society; to live from one pay-day to another—these and many other facts constitute the real problem of the proletariat.'

I give these quotations to show that there is now a school of professional economists which, some eighty years after Ruskin wrote *Unto This Last*, has reached the same conclusions that he did—namely, that 'there is no wealth but life': a strange political economy, as Ruskin then said, 'the only one, nevertheless, that ever was or can be'. 'It all comes down to the same thing,' says the present-day economist, in words less eloquent but perhaps more acceptable than Ruskin's, 'that even in the most ordinary aspects of life, for the correct balance of his volitions and actions, man must consciously or subconsciously be embedded in a vitally-satisfying milieu and be integrated into a stable and well-balanced community which is based on social sentiments and institutions.' 'It is social integration on which economic integration depends, and not the other way round.'[1] This same conclusion was reached by those practical sociologists who carried out, until interrupted by war and finally destroyed by post-war 'economy', the great social experiment known to us as the Peckham Health Centre.

Now that we have a definition of the wider social problem, we shall perhaps be able to see more clearly the relevance of that human activity which we call the arts. Among the forces making for social integration, art, in my opinion, is supreme. I know that the supreme place would more commonly be given to religion, and personally I do not wish, in this respect, to deny the claims of religion. But we are speaking here of life in its concrete manifestations, of man's work and the products of his work, of his material environment and civilized amenities; and though a moral factor does enter into all this, it is as the subjective aspect of an activity which in practice can only be realized through the senses, as aesthetic experience. I admit that this is a staggering claim to make in a sentence.[2] For many people, especially in Protestant countries, a sundering flood seems to flow between art and morality. I can only say, in this brief aside, that in my philosophy the two realms are not separable: the beauty of holiness is but the reverse aspect of the holiness of beauty. 'Beauty is truth, truth beauty.'

If, then, we recognize the re-vitalization of our whole mode of living as the real problem, we need not quarrel about the priority, or supreme importance, of one sphere or another. It is the life itself that is to be renewed, and all manifestations of this life, spiritual

[1] Röpke, *op. cit.*, pp. 70–1.

[2] It will be substantiated in a forthcoming book: *Icon and Idea: the Function of Art in the Development of Human Consciousness* (Harvard University Press, and Faber & Faber).

or material, will take on new form and colour. If we keep this statement of fact—for it is simply a fact, biological rather than merely historical—if we keep this fact clearly before us, we shall find that it will considerably modify our approach to the problems covered by the phrase 'the decentralization of art'. I think we shall find, in the first place, that the phrase is altogether inadequate and even misleading. The word 'decentralization' implies putting into reverse a process which has been going on for some time in the past. It implies untying a knot, releasing an over-wound spring, dissipating a clot—there are plenty of metaphors to give vivid actuality to the process. But the more realistic our notion of the process becomes, the less applicable it is in my opinion, to those manifestations of vital energy which we call art. Art, in short, is not something which can be ladled out from a glorified soup-kitchen, even if that institution is presided over by a Minister of Fine Arts. Art, in fact, as between one person and another, is not something which can be handed out on a plate of any kind. Art must be discovered, not received. It must be created, not conferred. It must arise spontaneously in persons and among groups, as an expression of their vitality.

The attempts so far made, with state aid and under official direction, to decentralize the arts, proceed on the principle of *diffusion*. They accept, as a bounty, the concentration of artists and works of art in metropolitan centres, and they aim to give from this bounty such crumbs as the starving provinces are content to receive. As an expedient, directed to the desperate state of aesthetic devitalization which exists in the provinces, the policy of a body like the Arts Council of Great Britain may be acceptable. The starving towns and villages of England should be grateful for the crumbs, and even substantial crusts, which have been thrown to them. But what these towns and villages require is that they should be enabled to earn the bread of art by the labour of their own hands.

The Decentralization of Art

The people who live in our towns and villages should be artists in their own right, and not merely passive receivers, or even active appreciators, of a metropolitan culture. To ensure decentralization of art in this sense, something far more drastic than a policy of diffusion is necessary.

Before I venture to suggest more realistic measures of decentralization, let us ask ourselves how the centralization of the arts came about. The process began in the sixteenth century, and was, of course, but one aspect of vast economic changes. There had previously been a centralized art of one kind—the art associated with the royal courts. But courts were not very stable institutions in those days: they moved from town to town, and did not necessarily excel, in wealth and works, the estates of the feudal barons. The king was but one more patron, along with his barons and the church. The essential life was the regional life, even the local life, and art was the direct expression of the social vitality and integrity of these dispersed groups.

The first stage in the centralization of the arts was a direct consequence of the concentration of power in the hands of the king. First the feudal barons and then the monasteries lost their capacity to act as patrons of the arts. During the thirteenth and fourteenth centuries the city corporations and craft guilds maintained a communal and regional basis for the arts, but this in its turn was gradually undermined by the growth of private enterprise and capitalism. To private enterprise corresponded personal patronage, which was prevalent during the sixteenth and seventeenth centuries. Its growth gradually reduced crown patronage to relative insignificance. The next stage was the commercialization of art itself. Art became a trade, or at best a profession. The author addressed himself directly to the public, and sold his writings to that public through the medium of a bookseller or publisher; the painter became a portraitist or engraver with the art-dealer as middle-man;

the musician a public entertainer, presented by his impresario. When that stage was reached, the centralization of the arts was economically inevitable.

The later phases of this evolution are best seen in the art of drama, and drama, if it may be dramatized, can by said to play the leading rôle. There are three stages in its evolution. First, the medieval miracle and morality plays, which like all the art of the Middle Ages, were local in origin and execution, local in patronage and appreciation. It is true that strolling players, forerunners of the modern repertory company, appeared as early as the twelfth century, but they were frowned upon by the Church. Then comes the stage of private patronage—a company of players maintained by the court or by some rich aristocrat, or powerful official—the lord chamberlain or lord admiral. The companies thus maintained by private patronage might travel, and indeed some of the English companies travelled as far afield as Germany and the Lowlands. Then from this stage of dependence on the private patron the theatre, during the seventeenth century, gradually emancipates itself, to become a private enterprise and to depend directly for its maintenance on the public.

Already during the stage of private patronage, the process of centralization sets in, mainly as a consequence of the stabilization of the court, the creation of a national metropolis, and the concentric tendencies inherent in a capitalist economy. But this process, which was to some extent arbitrary and uncertain under private patronage, became inexorable when once the theatre had been commercialized. For then a snowballing process sets in, which means that in order to make ends meet, the size of the audience must progressively increase, more must be offered to a wider audience in the way of naturalism and ostentation, costs go up, rents go up, competition becomes cut-throat, and we end up where we are today, all in Shaftesbury Avenue or Broadway.

This is admittedly a very broad description of an historical development which has much varied detail and many fruitful by-ways. But as a broad description it includes the essential facts, and will serve as a clue to some melancholy consequences. I think we might say that the tendencies set up by the drama gave a direction and a pace to all the other arts. Drama is the most social of the arts: it brings people together. It is also the most complex of the arts and involves, not merely the poet or playwright, but also the actor, the painter, the architect and the musician. The centralization of the arts is a direct consequence of the centralization of the drama. I do not say that centralization would not have taken place if there had been no such art as drama: art would inevitably have followed in the wake of the economic forces which produce a national concentration of wealth in a metropolis. But drama gives coherence and definition to that process in the arts. It provides a meeting-place for arts which may have been attracted to a centre by forces which in themselves were diverse in origin or nature.

Once the centralizing process has been set up it gathers speed, and a centripetal force of attraction is created which the individual artist can hardly resist. By the end of the sixteenth century a musician might still find scope and contentment in some remote cathedral town, but it is inconceivable that Marlowe should have remained in Canterbury, or Shakespeare in Stratford. Good architects were born in Bath or Edinburgh, and were to stay there; but our greatest architect, Wren, could have found his opportunity only in London. Great painters are born in Norfolk or in Devonshire, but they come to London sooner later to sell their landscapes or get commissions for portraits. Poets, who should be as free as the winds, are also drawn into the central vortex and only withdraw, like Wordsworth, at their peril.

What we must recognize is that for one reason or another the centralization of the arts in a city like London or Paris creates an ambiance or an atmosphere that exercises an irresistible attraction on the young artist or poet. Who among us blessed, or it may be, cursed with creative aspirations but born in the provinces, does not remember a sick and desperate yearning to get to 'the centre of things'? Here in London or Paris, we imagined, was the only arena in which we could gain fame, the only gladiators against whom we could measure our own skill.

This state of mind may well be an illusion. In a metropolis we may, indeed, sharpen our wits and polish our manners, but we may lose more than our innocence. Before I explain what I mean I would like to glance at a few artists who by exception matured their genius away from metropolitan centres of culture, and who yet, by general consent, were great artists. I will keep to the nineteenth century, which is far enough away to ensure objectivity, and yet near enough to exhibit all the features of centralization.

In drama there is the outstanding figure of Ibsen. We may differ in our estimate of Ibsen's genius, but in the past I think our differences were due largely to the controversial issues which were raised in his dramas, and not to any purely aesthetic judgments. Now that the controversial issues have died, and even Nora seems quite a natural sort of woman, we can recognize Ibsen as essentially a poet and dramatist, and as one of the greatest the world has ever known. Certainly he had no equal in the nineteenth century. We are then confronted with the significant fact that Ibsen's genius was matured in one of the smallest and poorest countries of Europe, and even then not in its capital city, but in the provincial town of Bergen.

In painting I would ask you to consider the case of Cézanne. At first sight it does not seem to have much significance for our argument. Cézanne may be sidetracked as one of the lone wolves of art, and certainly he was aggressively unaware of a public, proudly independent of any kind of patronage. But Cézanne is inconceivable without his Provençal background: he grows out of that regional landscape like one of its olive-trees. His genius would have wilted in a metropolitan atmosphere. But his significance is only to be fully appreciated when he is compared with another great man born about the same time in the same provincial town of Aix-en-Provence—Emile Zola. Both had the same background and upbringing, and they were to be intimate friends for forty years. To draw out all the rich significance of this friendship would need a double-portrait in the manner of Plutarch.[1] It is a story of gradual estrangement, and when the break came in 1886, it was between one man who had remained what he was from the beginning— a native of Aix, simple, solid, unsocial: and a man who had become in the full meaning of the phrase, a man of the world—busy, pretentious, sophisticated. When they quarrelled, Cézanne explained to the dealer Vollard: 'No harsh words ever passed between us. It was I who stopped going to see Zola. I was not at my ease there any longer, with the fine rugs on the floor, the servants, and Emile enthroned behind a carved wooden desk. It all gave me the feeling that I was paying a visit to a minister of state. He had become (excuse me, Monsieur Vollard—I don't say it in bad part) a dirty bourgeois.'

That is another aspect of the problem which we might glance at if we had time—centralization vulgarizes the artist, for that is what becoming a bourgeois means. But for the moment I am only con-concerned to point out that Cézanne, who was the antithesis of a bourgeois, and was a very great painter, was never drawn into the centralized intellectual life of Paris. He was born and remained a provincial, with a provincial accent and a complete inability either to dress or behave like a gentleman.

I might quote many other instances of great geniuses who have

[1] It has been done by John Rewald in *Cézanne et Zola* (Allen Michel, Paris, 1937).

matured on the periphery rather than at the centre of our civilization—a particularly interesting example is Emily Brontë. But I do not wish to give the impression that I am defending what is called *provincialism*. A great artist is always universal, and transcends the petty limitations of his immediate circle. He may still speak with a provincial accent, but he speaks with the gods. Having been brought to admit by the examples quoted, that there is no necessary connection between great art and metropolitan centralization, we have next to decide whether there is any necessary connection at all between an artist and his social environment.

In an obvious sense an artist is formed by his heredity and environment, but immensely interesting as it is, we must set aside the individual and psychological problem: we are dealing with a sociological issue, namely, whether art in general is best fostered by a centralized and metropolitan culture, or whether it grows deeper and stronger roots in a regional soil. Historically the answer is clear: the greatest artists have arisen in an overwhelming majority in situations or under social conditions which we should now consider regional. The two greatest epochs of art—Greek art and Gothic art—drew their vitality from confined and relatively isolated localities, and even the art of the Renaissance, as Sismondi long ago demonstrated, was an art inspired by local rivalries. But personally I do not wish to press this historical argument: there is no historical inevitability about art: it is a human affair, an affair of the free will, and if metropolitan culture is capable of inspiring a great art, I see no human limitations that would forbid that consummation. But I do very clearly see material limitations, and I see no way of surmounting them. Sociologically, centralization spells devitalization, and that devitalization of the material forces of a country means a devitalization of spiritual forces. The brain does not function unless the blood flows.

In the extreme case, this is obvious enough. No one would look for a vigorous school of architecture in the depopulated Highlands, nor expect a great dramatist to be born in the American 'dust bowl'. But the provincial reality is not one of such extremes: it is found in thriving cities like Liverpool and Birmingham, Middlesbrough and Leeds. Why are these cities, culturally speaking, no better than the dust bowl or the Sahara? Why is no Ibsen born in Hull? There is a Bridie from Glasgow, and all honour to him, but Glasgow does not support him: his fortune must be made in the West End.

The failure of cities like Glasgow and Liverpool, Birmingham and Manchester, to support their own dramatists is not primarily economic: there is plenty of money in such places, but it is spent on entertainment, not on art. These cities fill their Odeons and Majestics to overflowing; their citizens flock to mass spectacles like football finals and greyhound races; they give less certain support to the touring companies which bring them second-hand drama from London. But they have no indigenous art, no creative spontaneity of any kind. Art languishes, like a prisoner, in well-guarded art galleries and empty, echoing museums, to the smell of mothballs and floor-polish. The position is not so very different in the United States, except that the guards sometimes carry guns.

Vitality will only return with a revolution which humanizes industry at the same time as it disperses industry: which gives the worker responsibility for the work he does and a deep satisfaction in the place of his work, so that when his work is done, he does not seek to escape from that place, but stays there in joy and pride. The modern proletariat has no roots: it is 'mobile labour', drifting like cattle over the land, seeking nourishment where it may be found. But art is born in stillness, in contemplation, at rest. It is the still pool that reflects its environment, not the running stream. The first thing to contruct, therefore, is a centre of stability, an anchor in this restless flood of industry.

Such centres will be a natural expression of the new society we imagine and work for—as natural as the church was the centre of medieval art. If it is argued that we cannot anticipate the spontaneous evolution of such centres, and must work first for the social revolution, I for one shall not press the case for partial and uncoordinated action in this sphere of art. But an attitude of ever attending on the revolution that is to come is the best way of ensuring that it never will come. I believe, rather, that we can and should take action on our isolated front. I believe, in short, that we should attempt, even now, to create active centres of art in the provinces.

I have suggested that the theatre was to a large extent the medium through which centralization was effected. I am now suggesting that it might also be the best medium through which to effect the decentralization of the arts. It is an art which calls for the living human co-operation of many persons within a community; not only for its acting or presentation, but for its appreciation and growth. We must have regional and local theatres, fed by local talent, appealing to local tastes. The dramatic instinct is latent in the people, it is the one art which has not been wholly destroyed by false education, it has not suffered the regimentation and pedagogic dehydration which painting and literature have suffered. The British Drama League and other institutions of the kind will bear witness to the wealth of local talent that even now exists in this branch of art. Establish, therefore, regional and local theatres, but on a basis, and with an equipment, which will enable them to become the agents of that wider process of revitalization which we recognize to be necessary. Let them have attached to them concert halls for music, studios for painters, film studios and projectors, exhibition galleries and workshops. Let the artists inhabit them, as active practitioners and exponents of their arts. Let the people come and go freely among these artists, as they did in the Middle Ages and in the Free Republics of the Renaissance. There should be no barriers between the people and the artists, for every man is potentially an artist, liable to be inspired by the sight of another artist working in a way in which he would never be inspired by the divorced product of that work. Then, perhaps, a little moisture might reach the dried roots, and a vital art once again flourish from the soil.

VII

Towards a Duplex Civilization

In an earlier lecture I was concerned with the problem of education, my hypothesis being that unless you have some system of education, or mode of upbringing, which quite naturally and inevitably instils into the general body of the people *skill* in the making of things and *taste* in the consumption of things, all other efforts to give *style* to the products of the machine will be in vain. In the present lecture I would like to be a little more specific—to discuss these problems in relation to the existing structure of our industrial society and to speculate on what changes in that structure must take place before our ideals—those values of which I spoke in my first lecture—can be realized.

I have already made my main point: I have ridiculed the notion that you can take a pupil who has had a miscellaneous education up to the age of fourteen or sixteen, and then begin to turn him into an artist, or, more specifically, an architect or industrial designer, by means of a more or less extensive course of vocational training, as completely false. The miscellaneous—multilateral is the more obscure word used by our educationists—the miscellaneous education to which that pupil has been subjected before he reaches the age of twelve or fourteen most likely will have destroyed that basic sensibility without which a vocational training in design is a mere waste of time. The education of an artist begins at birth: it is the education, or rather *preservation*, of virgin sensibilities, and these sensibilities are so important in all walks of life (not least in the moral walks) that a few exceptionally perceptive philosophers such as Plato, Schiller and Bernard Shaw have maintained that aesthetic education is the only kind of education that really matters. As Shaw puts it with his usual force: 'The education that sticks after school is aesthetic education. Such terms as scientific education and secular education are thoughtless nonsense: science transcends all pigeon-holes; and secular education means teaching with a cane instead of a creed. The classification proper for statesmen is into aesthetic and technical education.'[1]

Granted a basic aesthetic education, a pupil can be made anything of, a good engineer or a good accountant, as well as a good designer. If the stock is good, any variety of vocation can be grafted on to it, by an operation that is painless and unobserved. A sensible system of education would not impose vocational training at any arbitrary age: vocation would grow out of natural aptitude, and our object should be to devise a system which allows such aptitude to emerge as naturally as a stem from the growing plant.

Existing educational systems are not aesthetic, and only a minority who have managed by luck or illness to escape their deadening influences show any natural desire to become artists or designers. This minority can at present pursue vocational courses, but few of these have any relevance to the immediate needs of industry. They can, it is true, become architects, and architects have their place in industry. In the existing situation industrial designers have been

[1] *Everybody's Political What's What* (London, 1944).

drawn largely from the ranks of trained architects, but no one would maintain that an architect's training is wholly adequate for the industrial designer. Apart from architecture, the potential industrial designer can only be trained as an artist—which, if the word conveyed its right meaning, would be perfect. But in fact this means that a pupil can attend a school or college of art which trains him to become a painter or sculptor, or, alternatively, a 'commercial' artist, which term might include poster-artist, fashion-designer, book-illustrator or artist-potter. Never, so far as my experience goes, could the product of these schools immediately take his place in industry as the designer of a motor-car, a machine-tool, or even a domestic utensil.

There are, of course, the technical colleges and institutes, and some of these run, like a trailer, a course in art. The degree to which this course is integrated with technical education may vary a little from one institution to another, but the link is never vital. Art is an 'extra', and it often implies no more than a superficial acquaintance with the historical conventions of 'ornament' and 'decoration'.

Aesthetic education, design centres, colleges of art, post-graduate courses in industrial design—these no doubt represent efforts which might eventually seal off oases of order in the productive chaos, but I do not see any certain hope of salvation unless all these measures to promote good design are spontaneous expressions of a social conscience. That is a somewhat metaphysical way of stating the evident truth that a style, in the historical sense, can only arise out of, and be a reflection of, a specific social and industrial structure. Or more simply still, a society gets the style it deserves. The predatory capitalism of the nineteenth century got the style it deserved—the worst in the history of taste. There is no escape from this interdependence of art and society, of style and custom. You can have great artists, exceptional individuals, who rise superior to their circumstances; but the daily bread of things made and used is sweet if the daily life is sweet, sour if it is sour, and just stinking rotten if the basis of society is injustice and misery.

I do not pretend to know what kind of industrial structure will eventually emerge from the evident breakdown of laissez-faire capitalism, but it would seem that the only immediate choice in my own country is between some form of monopoly capitalism and some form of state socialism: most of the economists one reads or talks to seem to expect a combination of both systems, the essential feature being an 'economics of control'. Such economists do not ask for the direct supervision of industry; they would be content to operate through the central instruments of credit issue, taxation, export licences, etc.

These alternative systems of industrial organization are nowhere fully established: we are dealing with tendencies. This is true even in a country like the U.S.S.R., where the economic and industrial structure of society has undergone vast changes since the Revolution of 1917, and is still changing.

We should first note that these tendencies, in all advanced industrial countries, are both economic and technical. I shall deal with these distinct aspects separately, and first with the economic tendencies.

The general economic character of the industrial system of the past 150 years may be described as competitive, and is openly defended as such by economists like Robbins, Hayek and Röpke. Its structure was determined by the profit motive, and all the subsidiary activities of distribution and sale depended on whether articles manufactured could be 'made to pay'. We may have various opinions about the fairness and efficiency of such a system, but no one is likely to question this general description of its mode of operation.

About the general economic character of the industrial system towards which we are now moving, there may be some legitimate difference of opinion, but I think we can agree that all the various alternatives rely on some form of centralized control. This is probably an inherent tendency of the democratic system itself, in so far as democracy is identified with majority rule. But the control may be either industrial or governmental. If it is to be industrial, the whole field of production will gradually crystallize into a few powerful cartels or combinations, international in scope, and to some degree competitive with one another—the heavy metals compete with the light alloys, synthetic rubber with plantation rubber and the shipping combines, shipping with airways, coffee with tea, and so on. If the centralized control is governmental, it tends to be nationalistic and totalitarian—it comes into direct conflict with the internationally organized cartels and in time of war takes action against them. This totalitarian control of industry is, from the economic point of view, essentially practical—it may be combined with either a fascist or a socialist ideology. The monopolist control is also essentially practical and does not aspire to an ideology. It knows that an ideology can easily be created once its power is secure.

We may not like either of these systems—we may long to be back to the good old days of private enterprise and laissez-faire competition; or we may think, as I do, that there is still another system to be evolved, based on co-operation and mutual aid. But both these attitudes are idealistic, and I think that we are forced to admit that the only practical choice, in the immediate future, is between the totalitarian and the monopolistic organization of industry.

This may seem a gloomy prognostication to those who believe in democratic control, but how precisely can such control operate if it is to operate from a centre? We may enact anti-trust laws, as has been done in the United States, but such laws are operative within a sovereignty which is limited in territorial extent. The trusts will register their offices in Luxembourg or Timbuctoo, and operate through anonymous holding companies. We cannot control an international organization by piecemeal national legislation. But even if we suppose that we can—if we suppose that by sanctions and other forceful measures we can compel all nations to take action against the cartels—what do we put in their places? The most rigid state control. And what does this control amount to in terms of personnel? An exclusive civil service, trained in new technical colleges and universities. Our wartime experience has shown the impracticability of that solution. We are compelled sooner or later to import into our civil service that same managerial class, expert in the administration of big business, which would otherwise run the cartels.

The more we concentrate, the more completely we deliver ourselves into the hands of the managers, or, as we now tend to call them, the controllers. This group, whether working for a cartel or for the State, will give us the goods: they will promise, and will achieve, a higher standard of living for the worker. In return all they will ask of the worker is that he should surrender his freedom—his freedom of movement, so that industries can be scientifically located; his freedom of association, so that labour can be docile and flexible; his freedom of opinion, so that the worker can concentrate on the job in hand. And I do not doubt that many workers will be glad to surrender these privileges which never filled their bellies, for a future of high wages, short hours, cheap amusements and every man a car.

Let us now glance at the technical tendencies of our time. There is little doubt about their dominant nature. The Industrial Revolution, such as we have known it in the past, was essentially mechanical. From the invention of the steam-engine to the electric dynamo and the internal combustion engine, it was a revolution exploiting power, and took the form of a progressive development of more and better machines. For that reason we call this period of development the Machine Age. Combined with the economics (and the ethics) of competitive enterprise, the machine had little thought for its material. Exploitation was its motive, and the natural resources of the earth—coal, metal, stone, wood, organic fibres, etc.—seemed sufficient unto the day.

But all the time, parallel to this physical revolution, a chemical revolution was taking place; and, though it had many important applications to industry, it was not until comparatively recent times that chemistry began to take a lead and even to threaten the whole structure of the mechanical industries. Power is, of course, still an essential, but the direction in which this power is to be applied may be completely switched over—switched from the exploitation of natural resources to the elaboration of synthetic materials. Not all these new materials are, strictly speaking, synthetic, but all are, on almost every score, infinitely preferable to the old materials. Plastics can replace wood, glass, rubber, and leather; aluminium and magnesium alloys can replace iron, steel, tin, zinc, etc.; rayon, nylon, and such synthetic fibres can replace cotton, jute, wool, etc., and even eliminate the process of weaving. Hundreds of existing crafts are threatened with extinction. The chemical phase of the industrial revolution is going to be more violent and far-reaching than the mechanical phase.

We may have all sorts of political and moral objections to these economic and technical tendencies, but I want to confine our attention to their likely effect on design. It is an effect which is already partly apparent, but the final outcome is anything but obvious.

As far as the economic tendencies are concerned, we may be fairly certain that design will not fare worse than it has done under laissez-faire capitalism. The effect of the profit motive was always detrimental to design. Art was the first luxury to be eliminated in cut-throat competition, and the number of people who were willing to pay more for a well-designed article was always, from the market point of view, inconsiderable. It is not a point that need be argued—we have only to look at the dreary products of the system. All attempts to improve it—the Prince Consort with his museums and exhibitions, William Morris with his craftsmen and workshops—were movements against the predominant economic motive and were doomed to failure.

There have been, perhaps, some stirrings of remorse in recent years. Some manufacturers did begin to realize that, other things being equal, design would pay. The efforts of a century of propaganda were beginning to have some effects on the buying public, which was becoming design-conscious. But the lead really came, not from the typical capitalists of the past, but from the managers of the first public corporations and industrial combinations. When competition is cut out, when profit is no longer the dominant motive in an industrial organization, when, in short, public service is the guiding motive, then good design becomes a decisive factor —simply because it brings prestige to the managerial class.

Logically, the same considerations ought to apply to the totalitarian control exercised by the State, but the evidence so far is not unequivocal. In the State where totalitarian control has been most absolute for the longest period—in Russia—there is little sign of grace. Aesthetic factors were left out of the Five Year Plans. It would not have cost anything to put them in—but they were left out.

The evidence from pre-war Germany and Italy was more favourable to the totalitarian system. Both regimes were design-conscious, but both illustrated the ambiguity of such a situation. The design did not arise out of the industrial system, but was imposed on it and, if not political, was merely academic. In Germany, after 1933, there was a deliberate return to the heavy, solid style of the Bismarck era, tempered with some influence of that Graeco-Roman classicism which dictators usually favour. In Italy there was more originality and, indeed, some attempt to form a modern style. It was mostly confined to public works, monumental art of various sorts, and did not penetrate very deeply into the industrial system. In both Germany and Italy the change, such as it was, was forced—it never became a natural function of industry.

We come then to that other form of central control which is exercised by industrial cartels, usually of international scope. Here the evidence is more difficult to collect. As a matter of fact, these international combines have so far in the main been confined to the manufacture of primary materials—metals and chemicals—and they have not attempted to control the making-up of these materials into articles for the retail market. There is perhaps some exception in the electrical industry. Generally, however, a cartel like the Imperial Chemical Industries, or Du Pont and its subsidiaries, has been content to supply the raw material of, say, plastics and leave it to small manufacturers to make what use they liked of such raw material. The vulgarity of most plastic articles is explained by this fact. No research has gone into the design of plastic objects—certainly no research comparable to the chemical research which produced the actual substances.

There are signs, however, that this position is changing. The wartime concentration of industry is one aspect of the change. The desire of industrial combinations to extend their tentacles vertically as well as horizontally is another explanation. When the utilization of their raw materials becomes the concern of the cartels, I believe that there is every likelihood that we shall see an immense improvement in design. Design will become one of the functions of management, and it will be governed by the same ideals of efficiency which prevail in the scientific and administrative departments of the cartels.

In political economy we associate cartels and trade combinations of all kinds with a policy of restrictionism, and it may be that this tendency will have to be brought under State control, thus destroying whatever virtues the system possesses. But cartels are not the only restrictionist organizations in our industrial system. Trade unions, with their policies directed against the dilution of labour, are potentially and even actually a far greater obstacle to the improvement of design. One has only to read of the opposition which a great and original architect like Frank Lloyd Wright has received from the labour unions in America to realize the practical veto which they exercise on new materials and processes. Anything which disturbs the traditional hierarchy of the labour market has been and will be bitterly opposed by the trade unions. There will be a big fight on the issue of pre-fabrication, and every new process which brings to an end an old craft, every new material which makes an old industry obsolete, will be opposed as bitterly and as unavailingly as the workers of 150 years ago opposed the first machines.

I do not pretend to trace a clear line through the obscure jungle of industrial change which lies ahead. I see no future which I can anticipate with any personal pleasure—the managerial revolution, whether in its monopolist or totalitarian form, seems to me to offer but different names for an essential serfdom, in which there will be little liberty, no equality, and only the fraternity of the barrack-room. But I feel fairly sure that that barrack-room will have more amenities under monopoly capitalism than in the totalitarian State. Monopoly capitalism still preserves a competitive spirit, if it is only the competitive spirit of rival industries. The fight between gas and electricity, between aluminium and steel, between plastics and a hundred materials, is a fight in which cost will be reduced to an absolute minimum and quality will tell as it never has told in the fight between private enterprises and national interests. The fight between industries is more promising for the consumer than the fight *within industries*. The very totalitarianism of the collective State, on the other hand, abolishes all competitive spirit—it even tends, by pursuing a policy of autarky, to eliminate international struggles. The English automobile, for example, so long as it had to fear the competition of the American car, was spurred on to some progressive sense of design. Abolish this competition, unify production under State management, and what motive remains for progress? The State car would be a utility car, economical to run, possibly cheap to buy, but as dull as a blue book or a postage stamp, or any other typical product of existing State industries.

When I say that a society gets the style it deserves, the implication is that we lack a great style in the arts today because we have not yet evolved a form of society from which a style can spontaneously emerge. This is another way of saying that as a people we lack *taste*, and once we have stated the truth in that brutal way, we have put the blame where it properly belongs—on ourselves, on our present social structure.

In discussing the problems of industrial art, and indeed the problems of art in general, we have tended in recent years to adopt an attitude which is too objective. We have thought in terms of the *thing*, the work of art or piece of craftsmanship, and too little in terms of the *person*. It is true that we have said quite enough about the person of the artist, even enough about the psychology of the creative process which determines the nature of the work of art. But art is meant for communication, for consumption; and what we have neglected is the psychology of the consumer, the person for whose enjoyment or use the work of art is intended. What we have neglected, in short, is the whole phenomenon of *taste*, and we have even become a little shy of using the very word.

An inquiry into the etymology of the word itself would carry us into some interesting by-ways of history, but it is only essential for our present purposes to note that originally taste meant something very definitely physical or sensational: the actual process of testing by touch (the word *tact* is related to it), and, in the sense still normal, the act of testing the flavour of food by means of the tongue. It was with that physical analogy in mind that the use of the word was gradually extended to describe the reception and appreciation of works of art.

When in the eighteenth century philosophers began to turn their attention to the sensory experience involved in the appreciation of works of art, they used this word taste. It plays a great part in the philosophy of Kant, for example, who defined it as 'the faculty of judging (or estimating) an object or the representation of an object by an entirely disinterested satisfaction or dissatisfaction'. Such a definition does not carry us very far, but it was the disinterestedness of aesthetic judgments which attracted the attention of these philosophers. Back in the seventeenth century Leibniz had pointed out that whilst intellectual ideas were judged by their clarity, and knowledge depended on the distinctness to which ideas were reduced by philosophy, another class of ideas did nevertheless exist which could not be reduced to clarity, which were essentially confused and only accessible to the senses, and only to be estimated by that faculty which we agree to call intuition. An artist, Leibniz pointed out, could not always give a reason for what is right and what is wrong in a work of art: if pressed, he replies that the work he dislikes lacks a *je ne sais quoi*.

I do not think that the innate nature of taste has ever been challenged except by the behaviourist school of psychology, which challenges everything that cannot be reduced to ounces or grammes. In general, taste has always been and still is recognized as personal and fundamentally irrational. What an individual *likes* or *prefers* is that individual's taste: what the aggregate, or perhaps the average of individuals in any age or civilization likes or prefers, is the taste of that age or civilization.

The irrational basis of taste is recognized in the old adage: *de gustibus non est disputandum*. It has been universally recognized that taste relates to the sensuous and physical constitution of the individual, and that therefore it is not possible to argue with him about it—you accept it as part of his disposition, as something that can no more be altered than the colour of his eyes or the shape of his head. In other words, it is assumed that taste is an innate and not an acquired characteristic.

This is, of course, a popular fallacy. It is true that we are born with innate physical peculiarities, and these determine the basic nature of the organs through which we receive sensuous experience. It may be true that the sensuous reaction of the newborn infant have an instinctive rightness about them and remain instinctively right so long as the child is adapting itself in a purely physical sense to its environment: the child, that is to say, has the same kind of instinctive grace as the kitten or the foal. But from the moment of birth and during the whole course of its upbringing, the human child is subjected to innumerable influences which distort its natural development—the influences of a man-made and artificial environment, and the more profound influences of the complex emotional relationships evolved by civilization. To take an elementary example: an individual's colour preferences are not always, or even generally, based on direct sensational reactions. Certain colours have acquired associational values, and one individual may like blue because it is the colour of his mother's eyes, and another may hate it because it was the colour his baby brother used to be dressed in, or because he unconsciously associates it with the sea and seasickness.

These associational factors have been studied in great detail by psychologists like Bullough and Myers, and more recently by the psychoanalysts. We need not pursue this aspect of the matter here, though we should remember that what some people mean by taste is precisely such an accumulation of whimsies or predilections. 'In decoration as in clothes,' we are told in an issue of the magazine *Vogue* (September 1945), 'taste is opinion, never standard, but a conscious development that gives one the courage of one's convictions'; and to illustrate what is meant by this vague but dogmatic statement, we are told that 'Princess Gourielli's flat in New York is rather like a collector's heaven. Everywhere "irreconcilables" of Period meet in fabulous amity. . . . Princess Gourielli (who is Madame Helena Rubenstein) is a great and catholic collector with a splendid barbaric sense of colour. She has filled her London and Paris houses and New York apartment with objects that amuse, or interest her, resulting in a fine *tour-de-force* mixture of modern colour and period pieces.' The illustrations opposite this statement show what is described as an 'eclectic mélange' of 'Victorian chairs; chartreuse rug; on the pickled-oak walls a Rouault in needlepoint, three African sculptured pieces and two Picassos . . . the Spanish Colonial bookcase was a find in Mexico; afterwards lined with mirror to reflect a Bristol glass collection'.

This might be described as an extreme case of eclecticism, but the more timid and less barbaric taste which indulges in Queen Anne silver and Chippendale or Shaker furniture is not essentially different: it merely substitutes, for the 'irreconcilables' which it needs a certain courage to display, the 'perfect match' which is dictated by historical knowledge or a dealer's certificate. I have no wish to decry such acquired taste: it has created some very pleasant oases in the desert of our ugliness. But it can never transform that desert. It is a dilettante and individualistic affair, and has no particular relevance to our present inquiry. What we have been considering in these lectures is *generalized* taste, taste which is characteristic of a people or a period, of a class or a civilization. This, I think you will agree, is an aesthetic and sociological problem of some importance.

There are at least three ways in which taste becomes generalized:

(1) by social pressures,

(2) by economic processes,

(3) by material or technical discoveries.

We need not pay much attention to the third way. Obviously if a new material, such as plastic, is invented, or a new method of construction, such as ferro-concrete, is evolved, or a new method of production, such as machine production, is introduced, then the material limits are expanded: taste has more (or perhaps less) freedom of choice, more or less scope for indulgence. But it is doubtful if these material factors affect the quality of taste: they merely feed the taste which has already been formed by social and economic factors.

An orthodox Marxian would no doubt argue that the social pressures which influence taste are merely a reflection of the underlying economic processes. In an obvious sense this is true enough; but once the economic differentiations have been set up, then the way in which taste develops within each economic group is determined by factors which are not essentially economic.

An obvious distinction exists between the taste of the rich and the taste of the poor, but it is not a distinction which follows predictable or consistent lines. Simplicity, for example, which may be an economic necessity for the poor, may become the last stage of sophistication for the rich; and the poor, by a natural process of compensation, will have a love of ostentation, a taste which is the meretricious imitation of the rich man's taste. But nevertheless, certain distinct class standards do develop within a class society.

But then another complicating factor comes into play, one which shows the superficiality of any too simple economic parallelism. This is the force of *tradition*. If the rich man could acquire his taste as simply as he acquires his riches, there would be no difference between, say, the taste of a successful manufacturer of pills and that of an aristocratic landowner. But the successful *parvenu* (admittedly there are a few exceptions) is probably a man who could only have gained his riches by virtue of his aesthetic insensibility. He is rich, but vulgar; and the one thing he cannot buy with his money is an instinctive feeling for beauty.

In his dilemma he is helped to some extent by *fashion*. He finds that 'the best people' furnish their houses with Chippendale furniture, seventeenth-century Dutch pictures, Persian rugs; he may even perceive that a minority among the best people collect less obvious things, 'Empire' furniture, impressionist paintings, or Chinese porcelain. He can be selective in his imitation; moreover, he can even employ an 'expert' to buy these things for him, and that is perhaps his safest course. But within his heart he must from time to time realize that these things are not *his* taste, but only, as it were, a passport to social prestige. He may be honest enough to preserve in some corner of his mansion a 'den' or billiard-room where he is not embarrassed by *objets d'art* and can 'feel comfortable'—or perhaps 'cosy' is the word.

The traditional taste which some people possess by inheritance and others acquire during the course of their upbringing, is a complex cultural product, maintained by the inherent social stability of a class, and perpetuated by the educational system instituted by that class. The only coherent tradition today, which still survives in spite of the violent social upheavals of our time, is that standard of taste which was introduced into European society at the time of the Renaissance. The new middle-class or bourgeoisie which came into existence during this period found in the accumulation of works of art, and in the support of artists, a means of expressing their class consciousness, the power of their wealth. Taste became a visible sign of success, and once this link between wealth and art had been established, there was a tendency to stabilize the existing values. If, that is to say, a merchant of the sixteenth century had converted his wealth into the tangible form of sculpture of the Hellenic period, or paintings of the Florentine school, the 'taste' thus expressed became a vested interest and as such was passed down from father to son. Moreover, the whole system of education was influenced in the same direction, so that the sons in question, and the younger generations as a whole, in so far as they were educated, were taught to appreciate the 'values' of such accumulated possessions. Academies were formed to perpetuate these same values in the practice of future artists, and the eventual result was an academic tradition strictly graded to the prevailing economic order, imitative and not originative in its ideals. Taste in this way became an intellectual category, a subject to be taught in schools; and the innate sensibility of the individual was trained to conform to this traditional standard. Sensibility as a spontaneous function only survived in folk art and in savage art—in the art, that is to say, outside the bourgeois pale. For a time, perhaps, we can trace the survival of the aristocratic or religious standards of the previous epoch, but by the seventeenth century it is already difficult to distinguish them. When an artist does by chance emerge outside the bourgeois pale (William Blake is the example that comes to mind) he is considered an eccentric and completely neglected during his lifetime. Later his eccentricity may be turned to good account by the bourgeoisie, for his works acquire the adventitious values of scarcity and antiquity.

As bourgeois society matures, it becomes more complex and divides into distinct groups or sub-divisions, and each of these may develop a minor variation of the established canon. Such subdivisions usually have either a vocational (professional) basis, or a regional one. The taste of the clergy, for example, is more ascetic than the taste of the landowners, and bankers may be more cultured than brokers (even when their personal incomes are comparable). Lower in the social scale, the possession of a television apparatus becomes a hall-mark of respectability. There is a subtle distinction between lace curtains and gingham, between plush and rexine, between oak and mahogany. More interesting, however, are the regional variations. These sometimes express a local tradition, originally derived from folk art (e.g., the tartans of Scotland), but in great cities like London or Paris they express the segregation which naturally takes place in large communities. Bloomsbury and Mayfair are typical examples of what I mean. The reason why intellectuals of a certain type formerly tended to congregate in that district of London known as Bloomsbury may be found in various factors—the proximity of the British Museum and the Slade School of Art, the existence of tasteful houses of the right rentals, the desire of like-minded people to live within easy distance of one another. This last factor is probably the only reason which brings together the fashionable set of Mayfair. But in both these districts, and in other similar segregations, we find the emergence of that intangible factor which we call *snobism*.

The snob is a social phenomenon of some pathological interest, but it is doubtful whether he has any real taste. His values are predominantly social and not artistic. But undoubtedly there exists a sub-variety which we call the artistic snob, and again he is a complex growth, typical of an ingrown and sophisticated civilization. He is a great hindrance to the true appreciation of art, not so much because he extols false values but rather because he is apt to fix on real values for the wrong reasons. Like the dilettante, he may have real sensibility, but he can only exercise it within a socially-approved range. He is fairly safe in relation to the past, for there he has the aid of the educational conventions already mentioned. But in relation to his contemporaries he must play an agile game, for artists are usually approved or disapproved for reasons which have little to do with the quality of their work. A good artist may be a bad 'mixer', a social boor, or merely a dull conversationalist, or he may have an inconvenient wife. Whatever the interest of his work, the fashion will turn against him and he will remain poor and undistinguished until a future age, to which his personality is a matter of indifference, re-discovers him. Contrariwise, many an inferior artist is exalted far above his merits during his lifetime simply because he is socially charming, or has made a good marriage.

All these considerations may be commonplace, but they show the difficulties which beset anyone who would exercise a natural taste. If such a person is an average member of our present society, he will have to contend against the following forces:

(*a*) acquired prejudices, chiefly those absorbed at school, through literature, the Press, and the film;

(*b*) inherited possessions. All but the very poor inherit bad furniture, bad pictures, tasteless or positively ugly objects of all kinds. To sacrifice such things may be economically impossible, or sentimentally undesirable. Many possessions which we value for their associations may be aesthetically disgusting. To be surrounded by such things may eventually corrupt our taste, making us indifferent to everything we possess;

(*c*) our environment. Our civilization has gone from bad to worse, until a point has been reached where the greater part of humanity live in surroundings which deaden their sensibility and reduce them to an apathetic acceptance of whatever is offered to them by the prevailing commercial system.

Generally speaking, we exist, as a civilization, in a state of frustrated sensibility. We simply have no taste, except bad taste. To get out of this state, some very drastic measures of reform will obviously be necessary.

I have tried to give you a realistic picture of the problems of style, taste, and design as they emerge from the prevailing tendencies of the industrial system, and you may not find it a very cheerful picture. But I am now going to ask you to assume that any defects in the prevailing economic system have been removed, and that there are no further obstacles to the full and free application of design to the products of the industry. Production is for use rather than profit, everything is made fit for the purpose it is to serve, and everyone has the necessary means to acquire the essentials of a decent life at the highest level of cultivated taste. Of course, there will still be plenty of problems left—those problems of individual taste and periodic fashion which I have already discussed. But virtually we shall have, not only a machine age, but also, what we have so far lacked, a machine art. It is, let me emphasize, a very possible Utopia. The necessary steps can be clearly defined and the only obstacles could be easily removed. The main requisite is a more flexible economic system, which will allow the industrial system to function freely without those restrictions on output and quality which are at present dictated by the profit motive. And there are many signs that the economic system is changing and will continue to change in this direction; indeed, it must change in accordance with the process of economic stabilization which is everywhere taking place and to which we must adapt ourselves if we are to avoid an unending series of world wars and the ultimate extinction of our civilization. All forward-looking economists and sociologists are agreed on this: a balanced economy is the 'essential foundation for the next step in human development'. I take that phrase from a recent pamphlet by Lewis Mumford, who continues: 'The conditions which favoured expansion during the last three centuries are all definitely over; expansion on past terms is possible only for the purpose of waging war. If stabilization should continue in purely pecuniary terms of monopoly, insurance, class privilege, the result will be self-defeating; whereas, if it is resisted, it must lead to a complete breakdown of our whole economy . . .'[1] Just as surely as we can forecast the inevitability of this process of stabilization, so surely can we predict that stabilization when it comes will be expressed in a general tendency to substitute qualitative for quantitative standards. If there are any laws of history (which I doubt), this is one: that a stable civilization is biased towards quality of achievement, a bias which has hitherto eventually led to over-refinement and sophistication. But that is the danger I am leading up to.

I have asked you to imagine that a stable civilization has been achieved, and that the industrial system is then devoted to the mass production of articles which satisfy the aesthetic standards which we have established for machine art:[2] economy, precision, fitness for purpose—the classical attributes of beauty. What then? We shall have factories full of clean automatic machines moulding and stamping, punching and polishing, innumerable objects which are compact in form, harmonious in shape, delectable in colour. Gone are the jointed and fragile objects which today we ingeniously construct from wood and metal: almost everything will be made from one basic plastic material, and beds and bathtubs, plates and dishes, radio cabinets and motor-cars, will spill out of the factories like an unending stream of glossy jujubes. I am perhaps exaggerating: if we get tired of glossiness, we can have our surfaces matt. Nothing will be impossible. The technologist and the designer between them will be able to satisfy every whim and fancy. From a technical point of view, it will all be fearfully easy, and we may well ask ourselves: where is the restraint to come from? What is to prevent this search for quality and variety from degenerating into an avalanche of vulgarity?

[1] *The Social Foundations of Post-war Building* (London, 1943), p. 20.

[2] Cf. my *Art and Industry* (new edition, London, 1945).

Prophets have a pre-emptive right to be gloomy, and in that role I would warn you that nothing whatever can save us from that avalanche unless we take preventive measures now. The children who are being educated in our schools today are the people who will inherit the Plastic Age we are preparing, and what powers of resistance will they have when they enter into the glossy land of promise? They will have less than we have, much less than our ancestors had. For what is 'good taste' as opposed to vulgarity? Is it something which can be taught at school, like Latin or arithmetic? Something you pick up at Oxford like an accent? Is it something innate, like an ear for music or a passion for oysters? Before answering such rhetorical questions—they are not meant to be answered—let us glance once again at the historical evidence.

The most striking fact about the great epochs of art, as I have emphasized again and again, is their homogeneity. If we could transport ourselves into the sixth century B.C. in Greece, to the eleventh century in China, into the twelfth century in Northern France, the thirteenth century in Italy, the eighteenth century in England, we should find not only great monuments of art in the cities and public places: diffused everywhere throughout those lands, in houses and clothes, in ordinary objects of utility and ornament, we should find the ubiquitous stamp of a civilization. It would not all be refined: it might be rough in texture, even crude in conception. But it would never be vulgar. The shape would be good, the ornament appropriate, the colour harmonious.

Now, the usual assumption is that somehow or other the high cultural achievements of an élite at the top of such a society trickle downwards until they reach the lowest cottage in the land. But such a theory is not borne out by the facts. Apart from the absence of any means of diffusion, such as we possess nowadays in the Press and the radio, in mass production and mechanical distribution, the chronological evidence is all against it. The peasant art comes first—we can prove it in the evolution of an art such as Greek pottery. But more than this: I believe that the peasant art is there all the time until it is corrupted by influences coming from a more artificial class. What I want to assert, in relation to our own particular problems, is that good taste is always built up from a broad basis; it is a slow elaboration and refinement of instinctive activities natural to man, and this slow process is what we call a tradition in art. It is only in so far as the constructive instincts of man are progressively refined by application to specific problems of form and function that anything in the nature of an artistic tradition can develop. That is a difficult sentence to grasp, perhaps, but let me be quite clear. I mean that the fingers must feel the clay, the crisp substance of the wood, the tension of the molten metal; there must be sensuous contact of hand and eye with the grain and grit. Otherwise we have made a divorce between man's senses and man's artifices which has never existed before in history and from which consequences will flow of a quite unpredictable nature.

Such consequences are unpredictable only in their symptomatic detail: broadly we may say that the atrophy of sensibility which is involved in such a cessation of handwork involves the decay of our civilization—some of us would say that the evidence is already plain to see, that the decomposition has begun. Now, I think it would be possible to elaborate an up-to-date psychological theory to explain why this should happen: it is summed up in one of the most ancient of psychological maxims: *nihil est in intellectu quod non fuerit prius in sensu*, which means that the basis of intelligence is a lively sensibility. But there is another and even more familiar maxim which gives the common-sense view of the process: Satan finds some mischief still for idle hands to do. If by advances in technology, in machine-tool design, by factory organization, and so on, the human element is largely eliminated from production, then, apart from the problem of the adequate distribution and consumption of these mechanically produced goods—a problem which, as I have already said, could conceivably be solved by some scheme of social credit—there remains not only what the sociologists with unconscious irony call the problem of leisure, but this much more serious aspect of the problem which I have called 'the atrophy of sensation'. You might conceivably solve the problem of leisure, not only by employing a greater number of people in distributive trades and social services, but also by various forms of cultural entertainment. It is an only too credible possibility—a vast conglomeration of shop-walkers and civil servants, ticket-punchers and typists, their hands getting more and more refined, their minds more and more cultured. Even the peasant's fingers will have forgotten the knack of milking a cow, and the spade and fork will have joined the rest of the tools of the Iron Age in our museums.

It might be said that I have forgotten the designer, and the pattern maker and the machine-tool maker. But these people who may still be required to use their hands in creative contact with a material will always be an insignificant minority in any individual community, and quite unable to retard a general atrophy of sensibility in a civilization. No: if we are to go forward to the logical conclusion of the machine age—and I am not suggesting that we should attempt to arrest an historical process of such acquired momentum—then we must create a movement in a *parallel* direction, and not in opposition.

We must, in other words, establish a double-decker civilization. That is not so fantastic as at first sight it might seem. Such a phenomenon has, indeed, appeared many times in the course of history, chiefly in primitive communities where a secret art was practised by the priesthood in complete independence of the utilitarian or decorative arts of the common people. But the most striking example of a binary or duplex civilization is that of Ancient Egypt, and it is one which offers some striking parallels to our own. In the valley of the Nile there existed for many centuries side by side two types of art of entirely distinct character. One, consisting mainly of public buildings and sculptured monuments, was religious; the other, consisting mainly of paintings, small carvings and decorated vessels of various kinds, was domestic. The religious art was geometric, rational, objective, abstract; the other was naturalistic, lyrical, even sentimental. These two arts did not represent the highbrow and lowbrow extremes of expression within a social unity: they were completely divorced styles, uninfluenced by each other, almost unaware of each other (Figs. 21, 22).

A similar stylistic division has already become evident in our own time, though few people are yet conscious of it, and fewer still are aware of its significance or willing to draw conclusions from it. But surely between the constructive art of Gabo or Nicholson, the functional architecture of Le Corbusier or Niemeyer on the one hand (Figs. 23, 24), and what generally passes for art and architecture on the other hand, there is not merely a separation, but a decree absolute. Among that other part there is much that is merely bad and imitative, and I would not in any case wish to lump it all together in one category. But among it we shall find the naturalistic, the lyrical and sentimental modes of expression which correspond strictly in character to the domestic arts of Ancient Egypt.

So therefore we are already a double-decker civilization, though there seems to be some confusion on the lower deck. But now let us carry the comparison a little further. I have already, in my book on *Art and Industry* and elsewhere, formulated the abstract principles which should govern machine art. The art of the machine can never be naturalistic or humanistic: it is an art of geometrical proportions, of purely formal harmonies. Though my last wish is to exclude those intuitive faculties which only the artist can bring to bear on industrial design, its general character can best be described as 'objective rationality', which is a translation of the very phrase which a German historian of art has used to describe Egyptian architecture. 'The characteristic which speaks out most clearly in it as a phenomenon in general is that naked, abstract absoluteness of the constructive spirit in its cold grandeur, its terse decidedness, its renunciation of every superfluous articulation.'[1] That is Professor Worringer's description of Egyptian architecture, but it might equally well be a description of contemporary functional architecture. The spirit underlying Egyptian architecture and the spirit underlying modern architecture is the same spirit, and it is something quite distinct from the naturalistic or humanistic art which led a separate existence in Egypt, but which is being slowly eliminated from our own civilization by the machine (Figs. 26, 27).

We cannot, at this stage of development, oppose the machine: we must let it rip, and with confidence. Egyptian art proves that a spirit of objective rationality is capable of the most magnificent and awe-inspiring achievements. We can already see its potentialities around us, in the functional buildings which have already been erected in this country and elsewhere, and in some of the products of the machine industry. But do not let us make the mistake of assuming that a civilization can be based on rationality or functionalism alone. The foundations of a civilization rest not in the mind but in the senses, and unless we can use the senses, educate the senses, we shall never have the biological conditions for human survival, let alone human progress.

We must look forward, therefore, to some division of our human and social activities which will insure a due proportion of time devoted to manual craftsmanship. It would be quite impracticable

[1] Wilhelm Worringer, *Egyptian Art*, trans. by B. Rackham (London, 1928), p. 24.

to achieve this by any artificial interference with industrial development. We cannot select several industries—say furniture and pottery—and reserve these for handicraft. Such vertical rifts in the industrial system would lead to economic anomalies and social inequalities. They would divide the industrial world into a technological priesthood and a lower order of handicraftsmen. That solution might be possible under some system of centralized planning, but I think we can dismiss it as undesirable and as only partial in its effects.

But there is another possibility, and this is to make the division horizontal, affecting every industry and every individual, but only up to a certain point. In other words, let every individual serve an apprenticeship in handicrafts. I have already made my plea for the aesthetic basis of education; what I am now advocating is an extension of that method beyond the school age, into the period of apprenticeship, into the hours of adult leisure. If, between the ages of five and fifteen, we could give all our children a training of the senses through the constructive shaping of materials—if we could accustom their hands and eyes, indeed all their instruments of sensation, to a creative communion with sounds and colours, textures and consistencies, a communion with nature in all its substantial variety, then we need not fear the fate of those children in a wholly mechanized world. They would carry within their minds, within their bodies, the natural antidote to objective rationality, a spontaneous overflow of creative energies into their hours of leisure.

The result would be a private art standing over against the public art of the factories. But that—in our painting and sculpture, our poetry and dancing, our artist-potters and artist-weavers—we already have. That is to say, we have a tiny minority of people calling themselves artists. I am recommending that everyone should be an artist. I am not recommending it in a spirit of dilettantism, but as the only preventive of a vast neurosis which will overcome a wholly mechanized and rationalized civilization.

I make a further claim. The art of that completely mechanized civilization can never, if it is to be an art, arise from the purely rational solution of functional problems. The function, after all, always relates to human needs. Human needs, in their turn, are always related to a natural environment. There can be no artificial separation of art from nature, of the machine from its environment. The great air liners of the future will soar above the clouds, but their very shape and size will be determined by the element which sustains them. We can fly because we understand the natural properties of air; and in every sense, in every direction, we shall only advance on an understanding of nature. Let our children therefore first learn about the potentialities of nature, and about the potentialities of those senses by means of which they can give a pleasing shape to the products of nature. In this way the community at large will gradually acquire a spontaneous desire to give expression to creative impulses, and hands will never again lose their cunning, nor eyes their delight in colour and form.

Only a people serving an apprenticeship to nature can be trusted with machines. Only such a people will so contrive and control those machines that their products are an enhancement of biological needs, and not a denial of them. Only such a people will be secure from the debilitating effects of mass production and mass unemployment (miscalled 'leisure'). Only such a people, with sensations still vivid and intelligence ever active, can hope to form a stable and integrated society in the industrial world of the future.

Index of Personal Names

Index of Personal Names

Index of Personal Names

HERBERT READ

Herbert Read, one of the best-known of contemporary critics, was born in England in 1893. After service in the British Army during World War I, Read began his career as a critic. He has written extensively on both art and literature and is also a distinguished poet in his own right. Among his works are: REASON AND ROMANTICISM, ART NOW, ART AND SOCIETY, EDUCATION THROUGH ART, ART AND INDUSTRY, *and* THE PHILOSOPHY OF MODERN ART.

MERIDIAN BOOKS

Social Sciences, Psychology, and Anthropology

ACTON, LORD *Essays on Freedom and Power.* M12
AICHHORN, AUGUST *Wayward Youth.* M5
ARENDT, HANNAH *The Origins of Totalitarianism.* MG15
COOKE, JACOB E. (ED.) *The Federalist.* MG39
CRAWLEY, ERNEST *The Mystic Rose.* MG24
FREUND, PAUL A. *The Supreme Court of the United States.* M123
FROBENIUS, LEO *The Childhood of Man.* MG23
GLOVER, EDWARD *Freud or Jung?* M34
HARRISON, JANE ELLEN *Prolegomena to the Study of Greek Religion.* MG3
HARRISON, JANE ELLEN *Themis: A Study of the Social Origins of Greek Religion.* M145
HUTCHINS, ROBERT M. *Freedom, Education, and the Fund.* M31
JUNG, C. G. *Answer to Job.* M86
JUNG, C. G. *Two Essays on Analytical Psychology.* M28
KARDINER, ABRAM, AND OVESEY, LIONEL *The Mark of Oppression: Explorations in the Personality of the American Negro.* M141
LASSWELL, HAROLD *Politics: Who Gets What, When, How.* M58
LEKACHMAN, ROBERT (ED.) *The Varieties of Economics, Vol. I.* MG46A
LEKACHMAN, ROBERT (ED.) *The Varieties of Economics, Vol. II.* MG46B
LERNER, DANIEL (ED.) *The Human Meaning of the Social Sciences.* M64
MACDONALD, DWIGHT *Memoirs of a Revolutionist.* M56
MALINOWSKI, BRONISLAW *Sex and Repression in Savage Society.* M15
NELSON, BENJAMIN (ED.) *Freud and the 20th Century.* M45
PIAGET, JEAN *The Language and Thought of the Child.* M10
ROSE, H. J. *Gods and Heroes of the Greeks.* M59
ROVERE, RICHARD H. *Senator Joe McCarthy.* M98
SCHUMPETER, JOSEPH *Imperialism and Social Classes.* M4
SWADOS, HARVEY (ED.) *Years of Conscience: The Muckrakers.* M129
WILLIAMS, CHARLES *Witchcraft.* M62
WILSON, WOODROW *Congressional Government.* M27
ZIMMER, HEINRICH *The King and the Corpse.* M93

MERIDIAN BOOKS

Literature, Criticism, Drama, and Poetry

AIKEN, CONRAD *Ushant.* M148

AUBERBACH, ERICH *Scenes from the Drama of European Literature.* M63

BELLOW, SAUL; BOTSFORD, KEITH; AND LUDWIG, JACK (EDS.) *The Noble Savage 1.* M88

BELLOW, SAUL; BOTSFORD, KEITH; AND LUDWIG, JACK (EDS.) *The Noble Savage 2.* M102

BELLOW, SAUL, AND BOTSFORD, KEITH (EDS.) *The Noble Savage 3.* M113

BELLOW, SAUL, AND BOTSFORD, KEITH (EDS.) *The Noble Savage 4.* M125

BELLOW, SAUL, AND BOTSFORD, KEITH (EDS.) *The Noble Savage 5.* M136

BERDYAEV, NICHOLAS *Dostoevsky.* LA15

BERRYMAN, JOHN *Stephen Crane.* M131

BRADLEY, A. C. *Shakespearean Tragedy.* M20

BRENAN, GERALD *The Literature of the Spanish People.* MG9

BROOKS, VAN WYCK *The Ordeal of Mark Twain.* M14

BROWNE, E. MARTIN (ED.) *Religious Drama 2: Mystery and Morality Plays.* LA20

BURNSHAW, STANLEY (ED.) *The Poem Itself.* M142

EISENSTEIN, SERGEI *Film Form* and *The Film Sense.* MG10

EMPSON, WILLIAM *Seven Types of Ambiguity.* M11

FIEDLER, LESLIE A. *Love and Death in the American Novel* MG43

FOWLIE, WALLACE *Dionysus in Paris: A Guide to Contemporary French Theater.* M92

FOWLIE, WALLACE *A Guide to Contemporary French Literature.* M48

GRIGSON, GEOFFREY (ED.) *The Romantics.* M132

HALL, DONALD, AND PACK, ROBERT (EDS.) *New Poets of England and America: Second Selection.* M135

HALL, DONALD; PACK, ROBERT; AND SIMPSON, LOUIS (EDS.) *New Poets of England and America.* M50

HALVERSON, MARVIN (ED.) *Religious Drama 1: Five Plays.* LA10

HALVERSON, MARVIN (ED.) *Religious Drama 3.* LA27

HELLER, ERICH *The Disinherited Mind.* M66

HELLER, ERICH *Thomas Mann: The Ironic German.* M118

HIGHET, GILBERT *Talents and Geniuses.* M77

HOWE, IRVING *Politics and the Novel.* M46

HUXLEY, ALDOUS *Grey Eminence.* M70

KIRSCHBAUM, LEO *Clear Writing.* MG38

KIRSCHBAUM, LEO (ED.) *The Plays of Christopher Marlowe.* MG42

KNIGHT, G. WILSON *The Wheel of Fire.* M43

LOWELL, ROBERT *Lord Weary's Castle* and *The Mills of the Kavanaughs.* M107

MAUROIS, ANDRÉ *Proust: A Biography.* M54

MAYAKOVSKY, VLADIMIR *The Bedbug and Selected Poetry.* M94

New Directions 15: International Issue. M18

O'BRIEN, JUSTIN (ED.) *From the N.R.F.* MG20

PACIFICI, SERGIO *A Guide to Contemporary Italian Literature.* M122

PASTERNAK, BORIS *I Remember.* M100

PRAZ, MARIO *The Romantic Agony.* MG5

RAHV, PHILIP (ED.) *Literature in America.* MG11

RIVIÈRE, JACQUES *The Ideal Reader.* M103

ROSE, H. J. *Outlines of Classical Literature.* M119

STANISLAVSKI, CONSTANTIN *My Life in Art.* MG4

TATE, ALLEN *The Man of Letters in the Modern World.* M13

TRILLING, LIONEL *Matthew Arnold.* M19

WINTERS, YVOR *On Modern Poets.* M73

Meridian Books are published by The World Publishing Company, Cleveland and New York. For a free Meridian catalogue write to Dept. AM, Meridian Books, 119 West 57th Street, N.Y.

Meridian Books are published by The World Publishing Company, Cleveland and New York. For a free Meridian catalogue write to Dept. AM, Meridian Books, 119 West 57th Street, N.Y.